TERRY & ME

The Inside Story of Terry Fox's Marathon of Hope

Kari I cannot thank you enough for all you have done for the success of the book

You are a great person

Bill

Bill Vigars
with Ian Harvey

sh.
SUTHERLAND HOUSE
Toronto, 2023

Sutherland House
416 Moore Ave., Suite 205
Toronto, ON M4G 1C9

First edition, August 2023

If you are interested in inviting one of our authors to a live event or
media appearance, please contact sranasinghe@sutherlandhousebooks.com
and visit our website at sutherlandhousebooks.com for more
information about our authors and their schedules.

We acknowledge the support of the Government of Canada.

Manufactured in Canada
Cover designed by Lena Yang and Jordan Lunn
Photo layout designed by Karl Hunt
Interior cover photographs by Gail Harvey

Library and Archives Canada Cataloguing in Publication
Title: Terry & me : the inside story of Terry Fox's Marathon
of Hope / Bill Vigars with Ian Harvey.
Other titles: Terry and me
Names: Vigars, Bill, author. | Harvey, Ian (Ghost writer), author.
Identifiers: Canadiana (print) 20230457622 | Canadiana (ebook) 2023045769X
| ISBN 9781990823312
(softcover) | ISBN 9781990823527 (EPUB)
Subjects: LCSH: Fox, Terry, 1958-1981. | LCSH: Marathon of Hope (1980)
| LCSH: Cancer—Patients—
Canada—Biography. | LCSH: Runners (Sports)—Canada—Biography. |
LCSH: Marathon running—Canada. | LCGFT: Biographies.
Classification: LCC RC265.6.F68 V54 2023 |
DDC 362.19699/40092—dc23

ISBN 978-1-990823-31-2
eBook 978-1-990823-52-7

To my wife, Sherry, who urged me to share my story and supported me through this journey.

To my children, Kerry Anne, Patrick, and Jordan who have always brought me great joy and accepted my eccentricities.

To my grandson Clive, who has listened patiently to me telling Terry stories over and over. He will pass them on long after I am gone.

And, of course, to Terry Fox's memory. We are all indebted.

CONTENTS

FOREWORD

WHEN I TALK ABOUT TERRY Fox, usually, it's a story I know more clearly than anyone else in the group – it's one that's fascinated and held me since I was six years old, yearning to hear of Terry's progress each day and through my time creating a documentary film for ESPN about his run, *Against The Wind*.

Reading Bill's book deepened my understanding of the days that formed Terry's legacy – from the daily itineraries of the run, to the logistical manoeuvres of such a large-scale event. Bill's insights filled out so much more of the picture. I realize now how much Terry's sheer work as an athlete permeated my own approach to training and preparedness. The telephone pole-by-telephone pole perspective, the goal-determined planning to reach the outcome – I wonder how much of my own athleticism was shaped in those days anticipating Terry's arrival in Victoria.

It's difficult to put into words the inspiration Terry imparted to a young kid in British Columbia. If there is a unifying reason Terry's story is so captivating, so emotional to so many who hear it, maybe it's the incredible promise he built into the Marathon of Hope, not of a finish line or a legacy, but of the impact of our steps, together and all they can mean.

At the same time, we know no one can take those steps for us, no one else's body will be challenged by the wind in the same way and Terry, ultimately, ran alone. *Terry & Me* reminds us, though, that a few good people in the support van can make all the difference.

Here's to those who pave the way for us, those who run alongside us and those that carry hope forward.

– *Steve Nash Order of Canada, Order of British Columbia, Canadian professional basketball coach and who played 18 seasons in the NBA, where he was an eight-time All-Star and a seven-time All-NBA selection. Nash was a two-time NBA Most Valuable Player while playing for the Phoenix Suns. Also played for Canada and was general manager of the Canadian Men's Basketball team.*

CHAPTER ONE

"How Do You Watch Him Do This?"

W HEN I FIRST JOINED UP with him on June 9, 1980,
Terry Fox was fifty-eight days into the Marathon of Hope,
running across Canada on his artificial leg to raise money
for cancer research. He'd dipped his prosthesis in the Atlantic Ocean
at St. John's, Newfoundland, the eastern-most tip of the country, two
months earlier and filled a bottle with sea water that he planned to empty
into the Pacific Ocean at the end of his run, symbolizing the completion
of his sea-to-sea journey. Hardly anyone had heard of him at this time.

I had been sent as an emissary of the Ontario division of the Canadian
Cancer Society, which had almost turned its back on Terry's offer to raise
funds for the organization. We had spoken several times in the weeks
before, with Terry calling me in my Toronto offices from payphones along
the highway—this was before the era of wireless phones and email. I flew
to Quebec City on the evening of June 8 and drove out to Edmunston,
New Brunswick where Terry had finished the evening before. I arrived
at his hotel at 2:30 a.m. and, having no reservation myself, decided to

1

catch a couple hours of sleep in the backseat of my rental car before the day began.

At 4 a.m., awakened by the sound of a motel door opening, I got out of the car to meet three bleary-eyed young men. I introduced myself.

"Hi, guys, I'm Bill Vigars."

Doug Alward, Terry's driver and best friend, seemed a bit confused: "You're the guy from the Cancer Society?"

I guess I was not what they were expecting. To that point, they had been dealing with more mature (in every sense of the word) individuals from the Canadian Cancer Society. I hoped I wasn't a disappointment.

That was almost the whole of our conversation. Terry was eager to get on the road and start his daily marathon-length run. We piled into the Ford EconoVan. At 4:30 a.m., with a sliver of moon barely casting a shadow on the dark two-lane Trans-Canada Highway in the middle of New Brunswick, Terry slid the van door open. No words were spoken as the young man I had met half an hour before eased himself down to the gravel shoulder. He walked over and touched something on the ground with his foot. It was a plastic bag covered with gravel that either Doug Alward or Terry's younger brother, Darrell, had placed there the day before. It marked the exact spot Terry had finished his twenty-four miles that day.[1]

There were no shortcuts with this crew.

Doug pulled away in the van, leaving Terry alone in the dark. We drove precisely one mile ahead. Doug pulled over as a far-off train blew its whistle. The three of us sat in silence.

---

1   I have used miles throughout the book because that was the measure Terry used and marathoners continue to use to this day. One mile, of course, is 1.6 kilometres.

It felt surreal. In my mind, it was too damn early to be doing anything, let alone going for a run.

A transport truck roared past, shaking the van. There were rarely cars at that hour of the morning, only these eighteen-wheel monsters rumbling by. The drivers must have wondered what we were doing out there in the dark.

Eventually, from my passenger's side mirror, I saw a figure emerging from the gloom, running towards us at an even pace. He ran with an unusual gait, taking slight hops after each step with his good left leg to give his prosthetic right leg time to catch up. His torso rocked from side to side as he shifted weight from one leg to the other. He kept his arms bent at the elbow and his hands loosely clenched in front him like a boxer in training. As he got closer, I was riveted by the look on his face. He was intensely focused on the road ahead. He did not stop when he reached the van. It was like he didn't even notice we were there. We watched him pass and then drove off another mile down the highway. Again, in my side mirror, the runner faded into the darkness behind us.

At the next mile, it was the same routine, except this time Darrell jumped out and stood by the headlights with a small orange cooler under his arm, a plastic glass of water in hand. Terry stopped, took a drink, then headed off once more. No words were spoken. It was too early for everyone.

The routine continued and as the day dawned, I got a better view of what was already becoming his familiar hop-skip gait. I could see his face more clearly: calm, pained, determined, eyes focused ahead, starting at infinity. Again, it was riveting. His agony was palpable. I marvelled at how he was able to propel himself on that artificial leg. It was designed for running but even at the time it looked rather crude—compared to today's $40,000 or $80,000 prostheses, it looks primitive. My mind was spinning, trying to make sense of it all. We were only a few miles into the chilly Maritime morning and I was already in awe.

Each of Terry's stops at the van took less than thirty seconds and each of them was accomplished in silence. As the light improved, I started to see past the pain in Terry's face to the athletic strength he exhibited. I don't know what I expected, but it made sense. He'd been doing this almost every day for two months now. He'd already run over 1,500 miles at a stubborn, almost religious pace of just under 3 miles per hour. That took a rare combination of prowess and tenacity. These days, an elite marathoner might train for 100 to 140 miles a week. Terry was doing about 200.

I was thinking about all of this in the van. Looking ahead, the road seemed endless. Terry was headed for British Columbia, planning to dip his leg in the Pacific Ocean, a distance of about 3,400 miles from where we sat. To get there, he'd have to run through Quebec and Ontario, Canada's two largest provinces, then across the three prairie provinces and on through the Rocky Mountains—I couldn't imagine someone running through the endless Rockies.

I glanced back once more in the mirror. He seemed so lonely out there. Cars and trucks whizzing by, dangerously close.

What was he thinking when he came up with this idea? If you dig into the history books, you'll learn that a couple of people had walked or run across the country before he set off, but I'd never heard of anyone attempting the feat until that point. It struck almost everyone as a novel ambition. In fact, it seemed just short of insane, even before you factored a missing leg into it.

The goal of the journey was to raise funds for cancer research and ultimately find a cure for the disease. At that point, the money wasn't exactly flowing in. Terry Fox is now considered one of the greatest

Canadians ever, if not the greatest, with close to $1 billion raised in his name in Canada alone, but at this time, again, few Canadians knew his name. Ford Canada had contributed the Econoline Van and Imperial Oil was providing gasoline. Adidas had donated some running shoes. A couple of other companies had chipped in but we were further from Terry's goal of raising $1 million than we were from the Pacific coast, which was one of the reasons the Canadian Cancer Society had sent me out on the road. Somehow, I was supposed to help. But I couldn't think about fundraising in the van that morning. All I could think about was the figure shuffling along behind us on the endless shoulder of Canada's only transcontinental highway.

By about mile five, I turned to Doug and asked: "How do you watch him do this every day?"

He answered: "I don't."

So I just sat there with the sun slowly rising and the traffic picking up. Dumbstruck. And in awe.

CHAPTER TWO

"You've Got a Malignant Tumour."

A S THE MILES ROLLED BEHIND us and over the weeks ahead, I would learn more of Terry's story, his family, and his ambitions. I became his friend and confidante and also connected with his buddy Doug and brother Darrell who had agreed to join him on the Marathon of Hope when everyone else thought Terry was crazy.

The Foxes were a hard-working family. Terry's father, Rolly, was a switchman for the Canadian National Railway. He was quiet with an easy nature. He raised four children with Betty, who was more outspoken and had a little Metis in her bloodline. Fred (1957) was the oldest, followed by Terry (1958), Darrell (1961), and sister, Judith (1965). When the kids were still young, the family moved from Winnipeg to Surrey, British Columbia and when Terry was about ten, they settled in the idyllic Vancouver suburb of Port Coquitlam.

As a kid, Terry was the same person I knew as an adult and very much like his siblings: stubborn, curious, relentlessly active, and fiercely competitive. He played to win, whether it was table-top hockey, wrestling with his brothers, soccer or basketball. As they say on the sports pages, Terry was all heart, which turned out to be almost literally true: he was diagnosed with an enlarged heart, a condition that has cut short many an athlete's career and threatened to derail his Marathon of Hope before it started. Doctors feared the stress of running a marathon a day, as he was proposing to do, could be fatal.

While the Fox kids played whatever sport was in season, Terry's game of choice was basketball. He wasn't naturally talented. In fact, he was told he wouldn't make the cut on his high school team because his skills fell short. His coach suggested he take up wrestling instead. Refusing to take no for an answer, Terry worked endlessly on his driveway and in practice out-hustled every other player on the court. First to arrive and last to leave, he eventually muscled his way onto the team and into the starting line-up as the star guard for the Port Coquitlam High School Ravens. In Grade Twelve, he shared athlete-of-the-year honours with his best friend and training companion, Doug Alward.

Academically, Terry was a fair student. Not straight A's but good enough to get into Simon Fraser University. He studied kinesiology and thought about being a physical education teacher. He tried out for the SFU junior varsity basketball team and ran into stiff competition. But, again, Terry impressed his coaches and teammates by working relentlessly and never flinching. He secured a spot on the team.

In the fall of 1976, Terry drove his 1968 Cortina into the back of a pickup truck. The car was a write-off. He was fine, just a little knee pain, not enough to stop him from going to practice the next day. The pain didn't go away, however. Terry being Terry, he kept playing through it. Finally, the pain was too much to ignore, so he visited SFU medical staff early in 1977. He was given painkillers and told to rest. For a month, the pain subsided.

7

While running track that spring, the pain came back worse than ever. He still thought it was an athletic injury related to the car accident. Barely able to walk, he went to a doctor and was referred to an orthopaedic surgeon who took one look at his x-rays and knew something was seriously wrong. Terry and his family were called to the surgeon's office.

"I knew there was something wrong, oh boy, did I know," Terry told *Toronto Star* reporter Leslie Scrivener, one of the first to start ongoing coverage of his run and author of the first book about him, *Terry Fox: His Story*. "When the whole family came in and Mom put her arm around me. The doctor came in and just told me, 'You've got a malignant tumour.' I guess I was supposed to be upset but I didn't do anything. 'What's that?' I said."

Terry had osteosarcoma or bone cancer. I was festering around his knee and threatening to metastasize throughout his body. His leg would need to be amputated six inches about the knee and he would need to undergo chemotherapy in hopes of destroying any cancer cells circulating in his bloodstream. The diagnosis gave him a 15 percent chance of survival (now, thanks to research funded in part by Terry's legacy, the usual prognosis is 50 percent or better).

Judith Ray was Terry's nurse at Royal Columbian Hospital. She cried along with the family when the diagnosis was communicated and over the next few months, she formed a tight bond with Terry. I met with her a couple of times over lunch to help me piece together what happened at this crucial moment in Terry's life.

"When Terry and his family were told what the diagnosis was and what the course of treatment would involve, as you would expect, they were overwhelmed," she said. "As an aspiring athlete, he was about to lose a leg, and as part of his treatment he would lose his hair. And the disease could still be fatal. It was obvious Terry was someone who set goals, so I seized on that and said he could either let this horrible scenario run right over him, or he could decide to fight it with everything he had."

The night before his operation, Terry's high school basketball coach brought him a *Runner's World* article about Dr. Dick Traum, who ran a marathon with an artificial leg in 1976. Terry read it and a dream shaped in his mind. "I was lying in bed looking at this magazine, thinking if he can do it, I can do it, too," he said later.

The next morning, in the hours before his 8 a.m. surgery, Terry showed the article to Judith Ray. "Someday I'm going to do something like that," he said.

Recalls Judith: "The idea of a new way of being an athlete was born."

Everything happened fast. The operation was over in an hour. It would be a few days before he got a good look at the stump that remained of his right leg. It was "swollen, awful, in sad shape," he said.

Terry was eighteen years old at the time of the amputation. Post-surgery, he was assigned to the children's ward. "The doctor didn't want Terry in with the adults because it was mostly senior citizens with broken hips," Judith recalls. He was older than a lot of the kids, but "it was the best possible alternative."

Judith's influence was crucial. With his semester at SFU almost over, Terry wondered if he should drop out. She told him that "this was no excuse not to finish!" He could still do his assignments and complete his year with assistance from a tutor, and do it while he completed his rehabilitation, learning to walk on his new prosthetic limb.

At Judith's urging, Terry made up his mind that he would maintain a positive attitude. He was grateful for all the visits he received in the hospital and the cards and letters from friends and family and schoolmates but he wanted no one's sympathy.

"All the support I had from other people really helped me," Terry said to Leslie Scrivener, "knowing that all those people cared. That, and being really competitive. I decided I was going to beat [cancer] and get off my butt and show these people what I could do, and that I appreciated them coming to see me and that it was not all sad and gloomy. So I decided that I would do my very best, that I would try to recuperate as fast as I could."

Terry was fitted with a crude temporary prosthesis—basically a plastic bucket for his stump with a stick below—until the swelling from the operation went down. He put his stump into the bucket and as the children on the ward looked on, he began the process of learning to walk with the artificial leg and crutches. He was soon outfitted with a $2,000-prosthesis with a better-fitting fibreglass bucket and a leg hinged at the knee, a solid improvement on the temporary limb.

Weeks after his operation, he began visiting the British Columbia Cancer Centre to begin chemotherapy, a process that would require regular visits over sixteen months. The treatment was challenging and not simply because he was absorbing strong doses of chemicals, each round of which would leave him sick in bed for several days. Being in the cancer clinic, surrounded by other patients, many of them children, many of them desperately ill, some at the end of their lives, profoundly changed Terry. He saw the pain in their faces and how their families were suffering.

"It shook him up," said Judith Ray. "There were people in the same ward as him who had the same problem as he did, and it was obvious some of them were dying. That reinforced the reality of what he was up against. Even that didn't depress him. It gave him motivation to really fight, because he saw people there were really suffering. I suppose in a way it's unusual—he's a real natural fighter and worked hard for everything he's gotten or done—but there are a lot of people like that who, if you encourage them when they're down are able to maintain that thrust forward."

The experience gave Terry a greater appreciation for the value of life and compassion for those who weren't as fortunate as him in their fights against cancer. He felt a sense of responsibility towards his fellow cancer sufferers and he saw the value of cancer research—it was largely due to recent pharmaceutical advances that he was beating the disease.

"After Terry's initial discharge," said Judith, "he would drop by to visit me on the ward—about every six months or so—first of all to talk about the impact of treatment including his hair loss. He actually made fun of the wig he used. Later he came to talk excitedly about his sports successes.... I saw myself as a cheerleader, encouraging him in whatever he put his mind to and he continued to reach out to me."

While he was still undergoing chemotherapy, Terry received a phone call from Rick Hansen, a paraplegic then working for the Canadian Wheelchair Sports Association (he would later circle the globe raising funds for people with disabilities as part of his famous Man in Motion World Tour).

Hansen had heard about this former Simon Fraser basketball player who had lost a leg and asked Terry if he'd consider suiting up for the Vancouver Cable Cars wheelchair basketball team. It was a new discipline for Terry—he wasn't using a wheelchair to get around—but he was thrilled to be competing again. Even though his treatments had left him emaciated, he threw himself into the sport with his usual tenacity. He gained strength and his hair grew back, curly this time. He became an important player on the team, which won national champions in 1978 and 1979. For the 1979–1980 season, Terry was selected to the all-star team of the North American Wheelchair Basketball Association.

In addition to playing basketball, Terry mastered the art of running on his artificial leg. He started by simply walking up and down his driveway at 3337 Morrill Street in Port Coquitlam. By coincidence, he would run 3,339 miles in the Marathon of Hope. As his strength and conditioning improved, he started running up and down his street then graduated to the track at Maple Creek Elementary (now Hastings Elementary).

It was all uphill, figuratively. Nothing came easy but Terry and his brothers and sister had been taught by Betty and Rolly that there is no easy route to your dreams—hard work earns success. You can become whatever you desire, but you have to be prepared to put in the work.

As he trained, the idea of doing something like Dr. Dick Traum, the amputee marathoner he'd read about while waiting for his surgery, took shape in his mind and became an obsession for him. He shared the dream with Judith Ray during one of their visits to the hospital. "He talked about doing a fundraising run because he couldn't put the images out of his mind of many of his fellow patients who did not do well with their treatment," she said. "He wanted to raise money for research. He believed treatment could be better if there was more research."

What Terry had in mind wasn't a run around the block or even a marathon. He was determined to run clear across Canada. It was a formidable task, but he was an athlete and he set about preparing himself the way elite athletes do: he set goals, trained hard, and gathered support. He worked alone, without the entourage of coaches, dieticians, sports psychologists and other experts most elite athletes have today. After fourteen months in training, he'd built up the strength to reach his goal of completing a marathon a day.

It wasn't easy. His prosthetic limb was fine for walking but it was not built for running. With expert help, it was modified but it remained a crude apparatus by today's standards. As he increased his mileage, he suffered bone bruises and shin splints, among other injuries. It became a process of pain management. "Usually the pain came in different stages," he said. "A lot of times, the very beginning is the hard part. You have to take the first fifteen or twenty minutes to get warmed up. Then you get over a pain threshold. That's what I did a lot. You'd still have the pain and blisters, and sometimes it would get a little worse and then not so bad again, but it never was unbearable." He worked on his gait, searching for a new technique that would allow him to move comfortably, eventually settling on his now-famous hop-step-shuffle we've all seen in the videos.

Terry's commitment to his training impressed everyone he came across, including elite athletes. Jay Triano is one of the best basketball players Canada ever produced. He would later represent Canada in two Olympics and be drafted to play professional basketball (and football) and serve as assistant coach of the NBA's Toronto Raptors, but from 1977 to 1981, he was the star of Simon Fraser's hoops team and an undergraduate a long way from home. "I remember going out to the university a week early and going into the coach's office and feeling a bit homesick," said the Niagara Falls native. "There's a guy sitting there, he'd had his leg amputated at the time and it did so much for me. I forgot feeling homesick. I quickly bit my tongue. It turned out to be Terry Fox."

Over the months, they became friends. Jay learned of Terry's dream to run across Canada and, watching him work out, became a believer. "I was taking the bus up Burnaby Mountain at 8 a.m. to get some shots in early and I looked out the window and there's my friend wheeling his wheelchair up the mountain. I get to the gym and he would come in, wanting to get some shots in soaking wet. I thought 'this is crazy.' Then I'd go to the weight room and he'd be down there lifting weights. All of a sudden, this dream that was way out there and no one believed in... you know this thing is actually going to happen. Terry was actually going to do this."

By August 1979, more than two years after his operation, Terry was running ten miles a day. He began reaching out to organizations and companies that might sponsor his run across Canada. His buddy Doug Alward, a serious runner, signed up for a seventeen-mile race in Prince George, BC, that fall. Terry joined him, finishing dead last with a time of three hours and nine minutes, but he finished and trailed the last two-legged runner by only ten minutes.

Not long after he returned home, he broke the news to Betty Fox: "Mom, I'm going to run across Canada."

"You are not," she said.

"Yes, I am."

On January 2, 1980, Terry sent a remarkable four-page letter to Judith Ray that laid out the full scope of his vision and the reasons behind it, presented here for the first time:

It was real nice to hear from you. Things have been going super for me. My running has become number 1 for me right now. I am now up to 20 miles a day. Christmas Day was my first day away from running in 102 days. This spring and fall will probably be the most exciting days of my life. I am running across Canada to raise money for Cancer.

I plan on leaving in the beginning of April and finishing at the end of August. It is over 4,000 miles and I plan on running 30 miles a day.

I will never forget the terrible days I had while in the cancer clinic and I am very happy to have the chance to help all those people who now have cancer. I hope that I will be able to help not only those people with cancer but also all others who are experiencing emotional problems. You are right, I do believe in climbing mountains. I plan on doing my best to make this trip successful, not only the running part but also the fundraising part.

My confidence in myself has really grown because of my training. I have run through sores, bone bruises, shin splints, a cold and terrible fever, torrential [downpours], hail, snow and across ice.

This, combined with the fact I have now covered 2,400 miles leave little doubt in my mind that I can do it.

The one problem maybe sponsorship. I have applied at several different places, but have only heard back from Adidas and [not legible]. Both are going to help. The Canadian Cancer Society is going to start helping me with the fund raising and promotion. I really believe a lot of money can be raised if a good promotion job is done.

My basketball is still going good, but my schooling has suffered from my running. Not only is there a lack of time, but I am usually physically and mentally [sick] after my runs. So I am only taking one course right now.

It sounds like you are having a very exciting and challenging time. I have always wanted to travel but never had the time or the money. I bet you never have a boring moment or day while you are there. Do you ever get lonely or home sick. I guess your comrades have helped you with that problem quite a bit. Have you ever gotten used to the changes in the food and H2O?

Since I won't see you again between now and my run I would really like to thank you for all the help you have been to be. I think you can remember how much I enjoyed my stay at Royal Columbian. How many people can say that [they] didn't want to leave a hospital to go home. I give a lot of credit to you for my immediate strong attitude and drive. I can still remember the night when Dr. Piper told me I was going to have my leg amputated and go on to chemotherapy. At first it was terrible, but it didn't last long. I remember you telling me I could still finish my University and that I could keep in shape. I was too busy to ever go into depression or feel sorry for myself. Now I have the chance to help others, just as you helped me only in different ways.

Did you know that when [my basketball coach] brought me that magazine with the runner that night before my amputation that running across Canada actually popped into my head then. It took me 1 1/2 years to start running and I did get started because running across Canada kept coming back.

I am now at the point where an incredible fantasy and dream can actually come true.

I hope you are really enjoying yourself and that your work will have the influence on others the same way it has me."

Sincerely, Terry

CHAPTER THREE

Who is this Kid?

I STAYED WITH TERRY, DOUG, AND Darrell the entirety of that first day in New Brunswick. We had breakfast at a roadside diner, which was a sight to behold. Terry loaded up on eggs, bacon, pancakes, home fries, French fries, a piece of pie and anything else that would feed the energy machine he needed. It was much the same every morning and again at dinner at dinner. Doug, the frugal one, ordered a small meal, content on finishing whatever Terry couldn't.

The three young men seemed to enjoy one another's company, despite the rigours of the road. I would later learn that it hadn't always been this way. For the first month, it was just Terry and Doug and things went off the rails for a bit. They were as close as two friends could be and Doug would be with Terry every step of the way—he would guard him with his life. But, from the beginning, Doug, like just about everyone else, including Terry's parents, felt the whole idea of running across Canada was crazy and that Terry was pushing himself too hard. Darrell had joined them in May to alleviate the friction in the van.

We passed through a number of small towns that day, on our way from Edmunston towards the Quebec border. I saw firsthand how people reacted to this one-legged runner, this boyish-looking young man in sweat-stained shorts on their highway. It wasn't much different than how I'd reacted. Awe, often mixed with silence, or tears, or shouts of admiration. All he was doing was running, but somehow he was making believers out of people.

Towards the end of the day, around 5 p.m., we were in a parkette in one of those small towns. Terry perched himself on a railing and gave his little talk about what he was doing and why. It looked like the whole town had shown up. As always, he spoke from the heart with an authenticity that moved people. His message was clear: he wanted to find a cure for cancer, not for himself but for the kids he'd met back in the ward during the first round of his bout with cancer. There were more tears, more rousing cheers, more applause, as well as handshakes and those famous Down-East words of encouragement—"You go get 'em, boy."

Part of the reason I'd been sent out on the road was that our office wanted to know if this kid was the real deal. Was he sincere? Was he committed? Or was he just some kid on a lark? How closely did the society want to be associated with him?

It may seem surprising that we knew so little about someone raising money on our behalf, but that's how things worked at the Canadian Cancer Society. It was a bottom-up, volunteer-led organization. We had a national office but in reality, we were a collection of loosely coordinated provincial chapters. Most of the resources and volunteers existed in these provincial chapters. Terry first approached the society through its British Columbia branch, which quickly realized that his goal of running cross-country required the involvement of the national office. The national office agreed to sponsor his run but it wasn't in a position to offer Terry support on the road or funding of any kind—that would be up to the provincial offices.

Ron Calhoun, a General Motors executive and chairman of public relations and fundraising for the society at the national level, met with Terry and suggested that he call his run the Marathon of Hope, which was great branding. Ron also sent a short memo to the provincial chapters, alerting them to the run and asking for their support.

That explains how my boss, Harry Rowlands, executive director of the Ontario chapter, showed up at my office door one day with a memo in his hand from the national office. "There's a young fellow, an amputee, running across Canada," said the always dapper Harry, a former Bell Canada executive. "He hopes to raise some funds for the society. See what you can do for him." Otherwise, we didn't know Terry from Adam.

Sometimes our loose organizational structure could backfire on us. Most people don't know that there were two individuals who were going to journey across Canada to raise funds for the Canadian Cancer Society that year. The second was a man named Harry Crawshaw. Harry had introduced himself as an eighty-year-old who was going to ride his bicycle from Vancouver, British Columbia, to St. John's, Newfoundland, the opposite route from Terry's. Presumably they would have met up at some point in the middle of the country, which would have been a wonderful moment for publicity and fundraising. I had sketched a poster we could use for the occasion—"Welcome Harry and Terry."

We never used the poster. Somehow Harry left Vancouver and travelled 220 miles through the mountains to arrive in Kamloops in just two days. He then showed up in Calgary, covering a distance of more than 370 miles in a single day. Either eighty-year-old Harry was capable of lapping the field in the Tour de France or something else was going on.

Of course, something else was going on. Our Toronto office was informed that Harry had been spotted loading his bike onto a Greyhound bus. The next day, Harry's daughter called and said he was sixty years old, not eighty. That knocked Harry off the Canadian Cancer Society's radar.

Stories like that are not uncommon in the volunteer fundraising world and Terry, in all honesty, had given the society reason to be skeptical of him. As part of his sponsorship agreement with our national office, he was to undergo regular medical checkups for his enlarged heart and overall condition. Terry had already skipped two appointments and officials at the society were pissed off. They'd gone out of their way to make arrangements with hospitals along his route, only to have him blow off the checkups. That was the other reason I'd been sent out to meet with Terry. I was supposed to convince him to show up for his appointments.

After just one day with Terry, there was no question in my mind that he was the real deal. I had witnessed his grit and determination on the highway. I had seen him speak to those people in the parkette, coming across as honest, humble, and well-spoken. And I had seen the impression he made on those folks and others along the route. There was something infectious about Terry. He turned people into believers. That he was also a handsome young man didn't hurt a bit.

I thought about raising the missed check-ups with Terry on this visit and decided against it. I didn't have enough of a relationship with him and his crew to start throwing my weight around. I knew that his mother and father had already flown out to talk to him about keeping his appointments and if they couldn't convince him to do it, he was unlikely to listen to me. I didn't have the credibility. I was just a pudgy little guy who'd shown up in Edmunston with a bunch of Marathon of Hope t-shirts that had managed to both mangle the French translation of the

Marathon of Hope and spell Darrell's name wrong. So I just went along for the ride, getting to know the guys and what they thought they were doing and their daily routine.

It was strict, the daily routine. Up at 4 a.m., on the highway by 5 a.m. with the goal of completing twelve miles before 8 a.m. when he stopped for his big breakfast; a two-hour rest break and, with luck, a short nap; back on the road until lunch, followed by a longer break after which Terry would finish as close to twenty-six miles as possible on the day. It was gruelling—most people, like me, would be left shaking their heads, asking "how does he possibly do it?"—and there were no deviations. Clearly, it was Terry's run, and Terry made the rules. He was going to do things his way, and that included medical checkups.

At the Quebec border, I said goodbye and promised the Terry I would pick up with him again at the Ontario border. It had to be that way. As a staff member of the Ontario division of the Canadian Cancer Society, I didn't have jurisdiction to work with Terry in Quebec, although, as things would turn out, I'd improvise on that point.

I tried gently to warn Terry, before leaving, about what was going to happen in Quebec—or, rather, what was not going to happen in Quebec. Like other provincial divisions of the Canadian Cancer Society, Quebec was free to decide whether or not it wanted to participate in initiatives from the national office. It chose to focus on other fundraising priorities. It didn't help that Terry didn't speak French and neither did Doug or Darrell. I told Terry not to get discouraged, that we'd have lots waiting for him by the time he got to Ontario. Not everyone in Ontario saw it that way, however, as we'll see.

I then drove back to the Quebec City to return the rental car I'd "stolen" from the Quebec airport.

When I'd landed at the airport two days before, I rushed to the rental car kiosk to pick up the vehicle I had reserved. The terminal was deserted and there was no one at the rental car counter. I looked around. I waited and waited some more. It was getting late and I had a three-hour drive of me. I needed to get going so, out of desperation, I looked behind the counter and found all the keys to all the cars. I took a set of keys to a car that looked like the one I had reserved. I found it on the lot and drove off, leaving a note at the kiosk with my credit card and personal information, explaining my situation. Another instance of necessary improvisation.

Now I returned to the airport and found an agent at the rental car kiosk. I explained that I didn't have a signed rental agreement and that I'd essentially just taken the car. I laid the keys on the counter and said I'd like to settle the account.

"This is not possible," said the agent in his heavy French accent.

"Well, there is a car outside, these are the keys. The car was not there this morning and now it is."

"This is not possible. You can't do that."

We went back and forth. He was getting agitated. I tried to keep calm. He kept saying over and over "You can't do that," and mumbling what I think were swear words in French. I finally asked to see a supervisor, at which point, with great flair, he grabbed the keys off the counter and told me to leave immediately, with a few more choice words *en Francais*. I took his advice and left to catch my flight. I don't think I was ever billed for the car rental.

My mind was racing on the flight home. It was my job, as the director of fundraising and public relations for the Ontario division of the Canadian Cancer Society, to make sure every man, woman, and child heard his message so loud and clear that they would fall over themselves to donate to his cause. I was thinking about a million things at once. What type of reception should we arrange for Terry when he crosses into Ontario? Could we get a police escort for him? How could we make a big splash in Toronto, where all the national media outlets are located? Could I get him on national television? I knew that we needed to get Terry in front of much larger crowds. If we did, this thing could really take off. We could turn all of Canada into believers.

I was frantically writing notes on a paper napkin, my modus operandi. No briefcase, no notebooks, no real organization. Everything was just kept in my head.

I was excited. I could hardly wait to tell the world about Terry Fox and his incredible quest. I was thinking, by God, this kid is going to do it. He's going to make it all the way across Canada. He is most definitely for real, and this thing is absolutely going to work.

I was also overwhelmed. We were starting almost from scratch. The Canadian Cancer Society's Newfoundland and New Brunswick directors, Bill Strong and Stan Baker, had stepped up and done the best they could for Terry but both were essentially one-man operations. Terry had started his run right in the middle of the society's biggest fundraiser of the year, and Bill and Stan had been stretched. There was little in the way of public relations for Terry. Apart from a small flurry of news reports at the very beginning of the run, the media hadn't demonstrated much interest in Terry. *Toronto Star* reporter Leslie Scrivener took note of his run maybe once a week, usually deep in the newspaper on, say, page five of the third section.

And then there were Terry's expectations. I'd asked him what he wanted to do when he got to Ontario. He replied without hesitation: "I'd like to meet Bobby Orr, Darryl Sittler, Prime Minister Trudeau, go to a Toronto Blue Jays game, and visit the CN Tower."

That was quite a list and a little out of my league. I was a thirty-two-year-old public relations guy from small-town Ontario. I wasn't hanging out with hockey heroes and prime ministers. I hardly knew where to start. I only knew that I couldn't disappoint him.

I felt a little more confident about Terry's fundraising goal. He hadn't started out with a specific target, but on his last day in Newfoundland, in Channel-Port aux Basques, population 8,000, he'd raised $8,000 before taking the ferry to the mainland. That was a pivotal moment for Terry. A little further down the road in Nova Scotia, he'd decided that he would raise one million dollars. It was a huge sum. You could buy a house in Toronto for $50,000 in 1980. Yet I believed it was possible. In fact, I had a feeling that it might only be the beginning.

It would be up to me to drum up the support and publicity to help make Terry's expectations a reality. I scribbled away on that napkin on the flight from Quebec City, thinking about him back there on the highway, hop-skipping along. When I'd first seen Terry, it had been the grimace on his face that impressed me most. Now, having spent time with him, I didn't think about the grimace so much. I noticed the smile. He had a great smile.

It gave me hope.

CHAPTER FOUR

A Cold Open

I T'S CLEAR FROM THE LETTER Terry wrote to Judith Ray in early 1980 that he didn't just wake up one morning and begin his run. He organized it like a military operation. By early 1980, he'd lined up a donated flight from Vancouver to Newfoundland and grocery vouchers from the Safeway chain in addition to the Ford, Imperial Oil gasoline, and Adidas footwear. His family pitched in to host an event at the Port Coquitlam Recreation Centre to raise $2,500 to pay for expenses, a generous amount at the time.

Doug Alward has been coaxed into joining Terry as the van driver and one-man support crew. He wasn't 100 percent keen on the role. Reserved and introverted by nature, he didn't like press attention and wasn't comfortable with fundraising. He also wasn't sure he wanted to spend seven months—the estimated time it would take to run from St. John's to Vancouver—sitting in a van with his buddy. But his parents had encouraged him to do it, thinking it would bring him out of his shell, and Terry was insistent. Realizing that no one else was volunteering, Doug signed on.

Terry's parents and Doug weren't alone with their reservations about the run: the Canadian Cancer Society, too, was concerned, not because of Terry's cancer, which was in remission, but because of his enlarged heart. The last thing they wanted was for him to collapse under the stress of running the equivalent of a marathon every day on behalf of the society. That's why it demanded that Terry submit to a medical exam before leaving and regular checkups along the route.

A week before his departure, Terry was seen by a heart specialist, Dr. Akbar Lalani, a heart specialist at the Royal Columbian Hospital in New Westminster. Dr. Lalani gave him a full explanation of his condition, told him he was otherwise in top shape, and tried to talk him into running across British Columbia rather than the entire country. He got nowhere. Realizing that Terry would not be stopped, Dr. Lalani warned him to stop running immediately and seek medical attention if he experienced any dizziness or shortness of breath.

Terry just smiled and nodded. He had no intention of complying. He didn't mention to the doctor that he had already experienced dizziness and double vision during his training runs. "I worried that maybe there was something wrong," he said later. "I was afraid. But I just kept going because [the symptoms] went away. So I figured I was okay."

Betty, Rolly, Fred, Darrell, and Judith were on hand to see Terry and Doug off at the airport, along with Doug's parents and Blair MacKenzie from the BC division of the Canadian Cancer Society. There were tears and best wishes before Terry and Doug boarded their Pacific Western Airlines flight for St. John's.

With a local CBC crew looking on, Terry dipped his right leg into the Atlantic Ocean in St. John's harbour at 2:45 p.m. on April 12. Wearing his white Marathon of Hope t-shirt and grey running shorts, he ran from the harbour to St. John's City Hall where he was greeted by Mayor Dorothy Wyatt. Many months later, he quietly told me that the wonderfully eccentric mayor had insisted he don her official cloak of office for an official photograph. He sheepishly agreed to do it. After a few short speeches, she stepped forward and gave him a warm hug. Together they raised the flag of the Canadian Cancer Society before Terry hit the road in earnest.

I cannot image the sense of excitement and satisfaction he felt starting out after his long months and many miles of preparation. It was really happening for him. He began at a twenty-mile a day pace, running across the barren rock of Newfoundland. As he'd mentioned in his letter to Judith, he hadn't travelled a lot, even in Canada. He found it thrilling to meet new people and see kids on the other side of the continent playing road hockey just as they did back home. Newfoundlanders treated him well, frequently inviting the travellers in for a meal, offering them a bed or a warm shower or to do their laundry or clean their van. Many stopped him to take pictures, to chat, and to donate to the cause. The support, however, was inconsistent. He went five days in Newfoundland without a shower, sleeping each night in the cold, unheated van.

Terry was often tired and irritable along this stretch of highway, no doubt a consequence of the physical load he was putting on himself. He had trained hard, but his daily mileage was now much greater than anything he'd attempted before. He was often running in the cold, rain, and occasionally snow, always running in shorts rather than sweatpants so that people could see his prosthetic. Hills were a challenge for the artificial leg and Newfoundland has some formidable hills. The uneven angles on the highway's shoulder were another challenge for the prosthetic, making it difficult for him to keep an even stride. He tried to make light of these issues in his diary: "Having an artificial leg has its advantages," he wrote. "I've broken my right knee several times and it doesn't hurt a bit."

From the start, Terry was also frustrated by the lack of support he received from the Canadian Cancer Society. He didn't realize when he planned his April start that it was the organization's busiest time of the year. April is the society's daffodil month. The tradition of selling the yellow blooms to support of cancer research began in Toronto in the 1950s and spread around the world. It's almost a sacred rite for cancer societies. Oblivious to this reality, Terry was frequently passing through towns unnoticed. The volunteers who might have helped him were all out selling daffodils door to door. He complained in his diary that he was falling far short of his fundraising potential:

> I started to try to do whatever I could to let the Cancer Society know about that potential. I tried to let them know as best I could that I was dependent on them to have things prepared and set up before I got there. In some places they did it; in some places, they didn't. It was frustrating for me because I knew there was not only money not being raised but people who I could have inspired, people who could have learned something, were missing me and that was because of the Cancer Society.

The limp reception he received continued to frustrate him right across Newfoundland. The lack of attention was soon causing tensions between Terry and Doug. Terry wanted his friend to make publicity calls and arrange media interviews, which were out of Doug's comfort zone. Before long they were barely talking.

Doug was right to be concerned about his friend's health. Terry admitted in his diary on day fifteen of the run at South Brook Junction that he was pushing himself too hard. But he wasn't about to slow down:

I was feeling pretty good and the first two and three-quarters miles went quite nicely. Then, all of a sudden, I was seeing eight pictures of everything. I was dizzy and light-headed, but I made it to the van. It was a frightening experience. Was it over? Was everything finished? Would I let everybody down? Slowly the seeing double went away but my eyes were glassy and I was still light-headed. I told myself it is too late to give up. I would keep going no matter what happened. If I died, I would die happy because I was doing what I wanted to do. How many people could or can say that? I went out and did fifteen pushups in the road and took off. My head was light but the double-sightedness went away. At five miles Doug and I walked about it for a while. I cried because I knew I was going to make it or being a hospital bed or dead. I want to set an example that will never be forgotten. It is courage and not foolishness. It isn't a waste.

The wind and the hills had taken an early toll on Terry. The symptoms he experienced were exactly the ones that Dr. Lalani had warned him about, yet he did not alert the Canadian Cancer Society or a doctor. In fact, several days later in Cornerbrook, a number of medical specialists waited in vain for Terry to show up for his agreed upon 7 p.m. medical.

The citizens of Port aux Basques at least let Terry leave Newfoundland on a high note. Local organizers had managed to raise $8,000 in the town of 10,000 people before he'd even arrived. They raised another $2,000 when he ran through town, bringing their total contribution up to a dollar per person. Terry and Doug boarded the ferry to Nova Scotia with a sense of momentum. Unfortunately, Nova Scotia was even less prepared for him:

When we got to Sydney, Nova Scotia, there were two or three people from the Cancer Society waiting for us, and Sydney's a pretty big place. That was pretty upsetting because I'd made it all the way across Newfoundland and now I've made it to Nova Scotia, things were picking up. $10,000 in the tiny town of Port aux Basques, and here we are in big Sydney and there's nothing, absolutely nothing. Nobody even knew. It wasn't even in the media."

While still feeling queasy from the ferry, he made the rounds of a few radio stations and managed to gain the attention of a local CBC television crew. The CBC wanted to film him running along the busy two-lane highway, a reasonable request that turned into a disaster:

The CBC was filming me from the side... They were only going about five miles an hour when I heard this huge freight truck come barreling up and not slowing down. Smack. At fifty miles per hour, it hit the CBC vehicle, forcing it off the road, over a ditch and into the woods. One of the CBC men fell out the back onto the highway and rolled into the fitch. I thought he was dead. He was conscious but couldn't move. The other two guys were hurt but not seriously. The CBC truck was totalled and the camera equipment ruined. It was terrible. If I had been five yards further ahead, I would have been killed. If the accident had occurred 30 yards before, the two in the truck would have gone down a big ravine. We went to see them in the hospital. I couldn't run any more.

Several days later, on May 15, Terry and Doug reached Sheet Harbour, Nova Scotia. They were just over a month into the run and he'd covered 794 miles. The day started fine:

We parked in a beautiful location overlooking the sea. The ocean was much prettier today because of the sunshine. After my break, I ran until a lady from the Cancer Society in Sheet Harbour came to see me. They had a reception set up for me at 5.00 and wanted me to run with the school kids. When I ran with the kids, I really burned it just to show them how fast I could go. They were tired and puffing. All right! I met quite a few people who had cancer. A great reception, finally, in Nova Scotia. Today I was feeling dizzy and lightheaded again.

Terry called me that day from a pay phone in Sheet Harbour. It was the first time I'd spoken with him. My first impression was that he sounded tired—very tired. It was also clear that things weren't going well. What I didn't know was that things were blowing up right then between Terry and Doug. Terry was taking out some of his frustrations with the lack of fundraising support and the general difficulty of the run on his friend. "Once when I handed him water, he just threw it in my face," recalled Doug. The day before they reached Sheet Harbour, Terry wrote in the diary that "Doug won't do anything for me." He was carrying his own water bottle as he ran and making his own lunches.

An incident along the road hadn't helped matters. The van had a tiny latrine that needed to be cleaned regularly. That entailed removing a very small bucket, about the size of a mixing bowl, and gingerly dumping the contents at the side of the road. On one occasion, Doug had the misfortune to slip on the damp slope of a ditch and lose control of the contents. You can imagine where they ended up. It did nothing for the mood in the van.

After Terry spoke to me from the pay phone, he called his parents. He was in tears, desperately unhappy. He didn't know what to do about Doug. Betty and Rolly got on a plane to Halifax.

It took a few days and a lot of talking and listening but Betty and Rolly managed to sort things out between their son and Doug, encouraging each to appreciate the other's point of view. When he spoke later to kids at a vocational school in Dartmouth, Terry made amends with his friend: "I couldn't help but cry when I said how Doug had to have courage to put up with and understand me when I'm tired and irritable." To better keep the peace, Betty and Rolly let their youngest, Darrell, the light-hearted one, write his high-school exams early, skip his graduation, and fly out to join the trek. Darrell calmed things down in the van and lifted the mood.

They took the ferry across Northumberland Straight to Prince Edward Island on May 24. The weather improved—Terry by this time had a healthy tan—and the Canadian Cancer Society representatives in Charlottetown did what he considered "a fabulous job." A local radio reporter showed up to greet him when he set out at 5 a.m. on May 25 and covered the run all day. Terry wrote appreciatively in his diary: "What a tremendous support!"

He also noted another dizzy spell in PEI on a day in which he ran twenty-eight miles. He was pushing himself extraordinarily hard. His feet were blistered. His cysts were torturing him. As he crossed over into New Brunswick, he was running on a spare prosthetic while his primary one was being repaired. Its knee joint gave him trouble but he refused to stop:

After a half-mile I fell flat on my face. I couldn't keep my balance and I was struggling to make ground again. My foot and leg and back are all being overstressed to compensate for the malfunction knee joint. I didn't think I would make it twenty-eight miles, but I did and it was fantastic when I made it. I couldn't believe I was looking at the back of the van for the last time that day. We ran right through the city of Moncton, down the main street, and collected a lot of money.

Terry skipped another medical appointment in New Brunswick. The Canadian Cancer Society appealed to his parents to convince him to do his checkups. They had tried but ultimately threw up their hands and said he was twenty two years old, capable of making his own decisions.

His diary shows that Terry was still bothered by the very uneven support and publicity he was receiving from the Canadian Cancer Society. It was probably good timing for me to meet up with him in Edmundston. I think my enthusiasm for the Marathon of Hope and my confidence that we could rally the nation behind him lifted his spirits and gave him something to look forward to. He was not looking forward to Quebec. He wrote bitterly in the diary: We learned that there would be very little done in Quebec. Apparently, they can't speak English. Maybe they also don't get cancer."

CHAPTER FIVE

Disruption

THAT I WAS EVEN WORKING for the Ontario division of the Canadian Cancer Society was a bit of a fluke, let alone being assigned to Terry's Marathon of Hope. I was a long-time volunteer for the society in St. Thomas, Ontario, my home town, but I had only gone to work for its Ontario division in February 1980, a few weeks before Terry touched down in St. John's, Newfoundland.

My main task in those weeks was to co-ordinate with volunteers across Ontario to prepare for the daffodil campaign. I thought it was a wonderful organization that made generous contributions not only to cancer research but to everything from public education to patient transport to treatment appointments. While I knew quite a lot about the daffodil campaign, I didn't really appreciate what a large operation it was until Air Canada, which delivered the many thousands of daffodils across the country, flew me and Charlie Cliff, our Sault Ste. Marie volunteer chairman, out to Vancouver Island to see the flowers growing at Vantreight Farms. Not being a horticulturist, I had to take the grower's word that those were indeed daffodils and that those tight buds would bloom just in time for the campaign.

The trip impressed upon me how important the daffodils are to the Canadian Cancer Society and to everyone who cares about the fight against cancer in Canada. Tens of thousands of people volunteer every year and millions of dollars are raised (in 2022 it was $6.8 million). The project requires the full attention of the senior people at the society and its provincial chapters.

Perhaps that explains why the Canadian Cancer Society could not drop everything it was doing in spring 1980 to help some crazy kid with his cross-country run. It's not that people weren't unsympathetic or unappreciative. They were just busy with something that to their minds was much bigger: their key fundraiser of the year and a proven winner. Terry was entirely unproven and as far as anyone could see, probably a one-off event—was he going to run across Canada again the next year?

Even if you set aside the difficulty of coordinating efforts across provinces in a heavily decentralized organization, the Canadian Cancer Society didn't have the bandwidth or the volunteers to manage the daffodil campaign and Terry Fox at the same time. That he received any help at all in places like Newfoundland and New Brunswick was a result of provincial directors like Bill Strong and Stan Baker, and some of their volunteers, going above and beyond the call of duty to pitch in.

Also, the Canadian Cancer Society hadn't dealt with anyone like Terry Fox before. He's what we now call a disruptor. He had his own vision. He was working outside the usual channels to pursue his self-determined goals and, in the process, he was inventing a whole new approach to fundraising for cancer research. Instead of volunteers going door to door with pots of flowers, he was saying "Come to Terry."

His method was new: untried, untested, and untrusted by many in the society who were comfortable with its traditional, time-honoured approaches to fundraising.

I hadn't been at the Canadian Cancer Society long enough to be deeply invested in the old ways of doing things or to fear change. In fact, I'd been hired to shake things up a bit. And I'd had the advantage of having spent time with Terry. I'd seen him in action. I'd felt his commitment. I knew how he moved people. I was genuinely caught up in the unique brand of excitement he generated. I was convinced that if we could just get Canadians to see him and hear his message, something special would happen.

After leaving Terry at the Quebec border, I returned to Toronto and the Canadian Cancer Society's office on Bloor Street and got to work. I'm better with ideas than organization. My assistant, Deborah Kirk, was indispensable both to me and the Marathon of Hope in the months to come. I came up with a lot of ideas and Deborah made sure they worked and got executed. It was easy for me to make initial approaches to famous hockey players and other dignitaries; Deborah had to follow up with hard copies of formal requests—this was long before email—and nail down the specifics. I had a notion that we could light up all the electronic billboards along the Gardiner Expressway when Terry reached Toronto; Deborah had to formally contact each individual billboard owner, gain support and make arrangements. You've never heard of Deborah, but she held everything together, something for which she's never been properly credited.

One of the things that worried me most was the higher levels of traffic on Ontario's highways. Terry had his share of close calls even in rural parts of the Atlantic provinces. There would be no marathon and no hope if we didn't get Terry proper protection. We sent a letter to Jim Erskine, acting superintendent of the Ontario Provincial Police, asking for his organization's support and a police escort for Terry. I expected the request would work its way through layers of police bureaucracy and that we'd be lucky to hear back before Terry reached the border. Years later, I would hear from Jim's son how his family discussed Terry's needs at the dinner table:

> Father realized that this young runner had limited official support, and was viewed by many as a traffic hazard.... we collectively discussed the pros and cons of the OPP becoming involved with the Marathon of Hope. Not only would police assistance in the province of Ontario raise the image and financial support to Terry's efforts but the OPP could assist in a very public manner. It would raise good will towards policing but most importantly an OPP escort might prevent any potential dangers to such a determined young man in his quest to defeat cancer. At that memorable evening around my parent's dining room table, Father announced that during Terry's run through Ontario, he was going to provide a full-time and highly visible OPP escort for Terry Fox and his Marathon of Hope.

It was another of the many examples of improvisation and goodwill would make Terry's run a success.

Here's another. The morning after returning from New Brunswick, I was driving to work down the Don Valley Parkway, listening to my favorite radio station, CKFM. I enjoyed the banter between the morning host, Don Daynard, and a chap named Jeremy Brown who had a five-minute spot just before the 8 a.m. news in which he cracked jokes about the world of entertainment. To my amazement, his commentary that morning was not at all humorous. He mentioned that before leaving home that morning, his wife, Brenna, had handed him a clip of a Leslie Scrivener article in the *Toronto Star*. Leslie was still the only reporter giving regular attention to Terry's run. Jeremy talked about the kid with one leg who was running crossing Canada. He said he was so impressed with what Terry was doing that he was going to ask his station to get behind the run and he urged his listeners to join the crusade.

I pulled off the Don Valley Parkway and instead of heading to the office, I headed north up Yonge Street to CKFM at the corner of Eglinton Avenue in the heart of mid-town. It was still early and the station was not open. I rang the back doorbell and asked for Jeremy and through the intercom told him I was with the Canadian Cancer Society and I'd just returned from New Brunswick where I'd met with Terry Fox.

For the next hour, we sat in a coffee shop where I regaled Jeremy with tales from the road. At the end of our conversation, he asked if I could return at 4 p.m. that afternoon. He was going to see what he could set up. I showed up at 4 p.m. and was ushered into a boardroom where about ten men and women were waiting. Jeremy introduced Bill Good, the program director; Brenda Burns, the station's public-relations leader; Quentin Wahl, owner of Cadet Cleaners; and Jackie Creed, son of the famed Toronto furrier, Jack Creed. I had nothing to show them but two grainy Polaroid photos of Terry and my enthusiasm. I tried to convey to them how sincere and focused I'd found Terry and how he moved people when they saw him run and heard him speak.

I didn't realize it at the time but that was probably one of the most important presentations of my life. These people were *connected*. They asked when Terry would arrive in Toronto. I said he was about six weeks away, so around July 11. Before I walked out of the room, everyone had agreed to get on board. "Don't worry about Toronto," said Jeremy.

"We'll make it happen. Take care of the rest of the route." And they would deliver.

I figured Terry was about six weeks away. During my short visit to New Brunswick, he and I had mapped out his planned route on a big map in back of the van. Simply by measuring out an average of twenty-six miles a day, which is how you did things before Google Maps and GPS smartwatches, I was able to develop a relatively specific schedule for him in Ontario. His plan was to cross over from Quebec to Ontario at Hawkesbury, near Ottawa. We would have to make a big splash in the nation's capital. From Ottawa, he would run down Highway 7 to Oshawa. There was a string of towns and small communities along the way. Deborah and I worked out a plan to create grassroots welcoming committees for Terry at each stop. I felt that if we could get a major event in Ottawa and support all along Highway 7, we would have good momentum heading into Toronto.

Now it was time for some old-school, in-person organization. I jumped in my car and headed east with an Ontario Road map unfolded on the front seat. I hit Norwood, Havelock, Marmora, Madoc, Kaladar, Shabot Lake, and Perth on Highway 7. None of them was much more that a hamlet at the time—the largest was possibly 1,500 people. My strategy was simple. I pulled into a gas station and asked whoever I could find to name the best person in town for organizing community events. It might be a service club, such as the Lions or Kiwanis. In some cases, it was the president of the local branch of the Federated Women's Institute. I had grown up in rural Ontario so I was pretty familiar with how things worked. My only sales tools were a couple of Polaroid photos of Terry and my enthusiasm. I was excited to tell the story and could paint a good picture.

The response in each community was much like the one I received in Kaladar where a lovely person named in Glenda Bence stepped up to help. She was warm and inviting and not the least bit skeptical. "If he makes it this far, we'll do something," she said. I told her: "I can guarantee he'll be here."

As I was working Highway 7, two men in Ottawa were laying the groundwork for events in the capital. Canadian Cancer Society volunteer Major Terrance J. Christopher and Ottawa district director Jack Hilliard had taken matters into their own hands even before the larger Ontario division was fully onboard.

I mentioned earlier that the Canadian Cancer Society has a national office as well as provincial divisions. In Ontario, the provincial division is further divided into eight districts: Ottawa, Eastern Ontario, Toronto, Oakville/Mississauga, Hamilton/Niagara, Southern Ontario, Central Ontario and Northern Ontario. From the outset, Toronto and Hamilton did not want to be part of the Marathon of Hope. Given that they were the two biggest districts in Ontario, this was a major stumbling block.

The dissenting districts argued that the April daffodil campaign had just finished and they did not have the volunteer manpower available to mount another major project. One local office told us, "we'll be on holidays." I explained over and over again that the Marathon of Hope was going to be unlike anything they'd seen before. They were unmoved. I got the sense that some of the district directors simply didn't want to take on more work or responsibility.

Despite the lack of alignment, we forged ahead. Terry was approaching at the rate of twenty-six miles a day and we had a million things to do in preparation. We couldn't afford to waste time. We just hoped for the best and tried not to think about possibly having to tell Terry that the Canadian Cancer Society wasn't going to get behind him in the nation's largest province. We took comfort in the fact that district directors Jack Hilliard in Ottawa, Jack Lambert in Eastern Ontario, Bill Montgomery in Southern Ontario, George Carter in Central Ontario and Lou Fine in Northern Ontario were behind us. We might be without the two largest districts, but we at least had majority support.

Otherwise, things were going well. I was collecting positive news to share with Terry: Darryl Sittler had responded positively and we'd lined up the Blue Jays game and the CN Tower. Things were falling into place. I felt confident that we'd be able to do almost anything Terry wanted.

And then came the crisis call.

In retrospect it seems that the calls always came on Sunday evenings. This time it was John Simpson, the Canadian Cancer Society's audio-visual consultant. John had an extensive background in television. One of his credits was a writer on the CBC series *Wojeck* starring John Vernon (*Dirty Harry, Animal House*). He'd realized Terry's potential long before most other people and decided to invest his own money to follow Terry with a cameraman, Scott Hamilton, and various sound technicians. Way back in Nova Scotia, they had started shooting footage for a documentary. They picked up with Terry again in Quebec City, which was where he called from.

John's message to me was short and blunt. The three boys had run out of money. They had also used up their gas cards. All of them had colds and they had been eating poorly and sleeping every night in the cramped and smelly Ford Econovan. It was unhealthy.

John had just used his own credit card to put them up in a motel. "If you don't do something fast," he said, "this thing is not going to last another week." He was dead serious, his voice almost angry.

Things got worse. The next morning, the Quebec Provincial Police took Terry off the main highways and told him if he did not have a "Slow–Runner Ahead" sign installed on the back of the van he was off the road completely.

I immediately called one of my bosses, Ron Potter, the volunteer chair of publicity and fundraising for the Ontario division. Ron was an insurance executive in London, Ontario, and a former football coach at the University of Western Ontario. He was a wise and good-humoured man with natural leadership abilities. I explained the problems and he drove into Toronto first thing Monday morning. As he was driving, I met my other boss, Harry Rowlands, the full-time executive director of the Ontario chapter, at his office door and brought him up to speed. By 10 a.m., the three of us were together in Harry's office. What the hell were we going to do?.

Harry had a sly smile on his face and a solution. "Well, technically you can't go into Quebec to help. It's a different division. But if you want to take a vacation, you can do anything you want."

I mentioned that having just taken the job, I hadn't accrued many vacation days.

"You have to do what you have to do," said Harry.

So I did.

Deborah called a sign company and ordered a round metal sign to fit over the spare tire on the van's rear door. It would be ready late Wednesday night.

Another issue was that I didn't speak French and neither did the boys and it was making it difficult to solve problems in Quebec. I had to think fast and call in a favour. A good friend and former colleague of mine, Ray Bedard, lived in Welland, Ontario. He was young, free-spirited, and bilingual. I phoned him out of the blue and told him I might need him on a moment's notice: "If a vote goes the way I need it to go, can you pick up, jump on a red eye, and meet me in Montreal for a couple of days?"

"Sure, but what are you talking about?" he asked.

"I'll let you know if it comes together," I said.

I was ready to head to Quebec but before I left there was a big decision to be made—one being deliberated way over my head.

Rob Potter and another key publicity volunteer, Rick Smith, a radio DJ in Windsor, had called an emergency meeting of the Ontario publicity and fundraising committees, pulling volunteers from across the province into Toronto on forty-eight-hours' notice. The topic under discussion: was Ontario in or out of the Marathon of Hope?

About forty people arrived from all over Ontario and gathered in a meeting room at the Westbury Hotel on Yonge Street near Maple Leaf Gardens. At the time, it was one of the largest and nicest establishments in the city. Harry, as the senior staff member in attendance, said nothing. He worked for the volunteers, not the other way around, although I suspect he had made his opinion known quietly to a number of trusted people beforehand. Ron chaired the meeting. He, too, said very little. He let everyone else in the room express opinions. Representatives from the Toronto and Hamilton districts repeated their concerns about being over-stretched and their reluctance to back the Marathon of Hope.

My stomach was in knots. There was so much riding on the decision. It would make or break Terry's run. We would either be in a position to deliver everything I'd promised him and launch the Marathon of Hope into the stratosphere, or we'd be saying sorry, wishing him well, and maybe waving at him as he headed towards Manitoba. I couldn't bear it.

After all the back and forth, Ron Potter said his piece. He backed Terry vigorously. He spoke of Terry's fundraising vision. He related all that he had heard of Terry, his personality and his level commitment. He said he was ready to bet on the kid and that this was something the society just had to do.

The Hamilton representatives finally came around. The Toronto delegation, however, remained unmoved. A vote was called.

It passed, a huge turning point for the Marathon of Hope, not to mention for the Canadian Cancer Society, giving everything that flowed from it.

Harry turned, looked at me, and said, "Go!"

I ran out of the hotel, my gym bag in hand. I don't think I owned a suitcase at that time. I headed to the airport. Ray showed up at a moment's notice. Deborah found us in the terminal. She was carrying a large round metal sign that read "Slow—Runner Ahead," as demanded by the Sûreté du Québec.

We got off the red eye and in the early hours of the morning caught up with the boys on a secondary highway near Drummondville, roughly halfway between Quebec City and Montreal. We weren't a moment too soon.

Shortly after we arrived, the police showed up: two cruisers, one driven by a young officer, the other by an older gentleman with a few stripes on his uniform. They immediately ordered Terry off the road. I showed them the sign. It gave them pause but I couldn't tell if it had changed their minds. With my lack of French and their lack of English, we were at an impasse. I went back to the van where Ray was waiting and said, "You have to say something. I don't care what you do but you have to keep us on the road.

Ray had no idea what he had signed up for so he took no chances and showed up in a jacket and tie instead of jeans and a t-shirt. The rest of us were rather disheveled. Ray looked every inch the boss of us. It played into the ruse he concocted.

Terry, Doug, Darrell and I watched from a distance ten minutes of animated conversation. We couldn't really hear and certainly couldn't understand what was being said but our fingers were crossed.

Finally, the police shook Ray's hand, got back into their cruiser, and drove away. We were never bothered by the Quebec police again.

In fairness to the officers, they were really only concerned for Terry's safety. Ray said that the younger officer had mentioned before he drove away, "we just don't want to be called out for a dead body at the side of the road." In the short time I was in Quebec, I got a good look at the hazards Terry faced on the narrow two-lane highway. Transport trucks seemed to whiz by a foot or two from his shoulder. He told me that on one occasion, he dove into a ditch to avoid being hit.

I drove ahead with Ray, looking for a restaurant where we could all eat breakfast. Terry told me on the phone before I'd arrived that they'd been avoiding restaurants and other establishments because of the language barrier. Doug said that they'd gone four or five days without washing because they didn't know how to ask for a shower in French. We found a place and spoke briefly to the waitress, who was completely bilingual. We told her we'd be back shortly.

After watching Terry run his final mile of the morning, we told the guys we'd found a great breakfast spot. The three of them followed Ray and I up the road. We all sat down at a table and the waitress brought us menus and water.

The menu was all in French. Terry took one look at it and decided to give his order to Ray. He wanted bacon and eggs, two orders of toast, an order of pancakes, a milkshake, a large soda, and a piece of pie. It took many calories to keep that engine burning.

Ray, with a straight face, turned to the waitress and in comically broken English said: "Ee would like tree piece de bacon, dew egg, da yellow up, toast, much toast...." The waitress wrote everything down without so much as a blink. Ray then said something to her in French and she walked away.

There was a moment of complete silence at the table. Terry turned to Ray and said, "Are you telling me that's all I had to do all this time?"

He completely fell for it. The waitress returned and said to him in perfect English, "What flavor of milkshake do you want?."

We all had a great and much-needed laugh.

We were all so happy and relieved to be able continue the run through Quebec that it never occurred to me to ask Ray exactly what he'd said to the officers to save the day. More than twenty-five years later, over a beer in a bar, I said to him: "Remember when you spoke to the police that day on the highway in Quebec? What did you say to them to send them away?"

"Well, the young guy was much easier to deal with," Ray told me, "but when I started talking French to them their attitudes completely changed. They loosened up a bit. Then, I have no idea how it popped into my head, I told them that I was from the prime minister's office and I had been sent from Ottawa to assure that Terry would arrive in the capital for the Canada Day celebrations and I needed their co-operation and that of the force. They bought it."

Ray had done what he had to do. As we all did in the Marathon of Hope. Anything to keep it rolling and let Terry run without interference.

CHAPTER SIX

"I Love You"

TERRY WAS CHARMED BY QUEBEC. He had already seen a lot of beautiful scenery on the East Coast but nothing impressed him quite like the St. Lawrence River—"beautiful, so large... the towns are simply gorgeous." Quebec City was magnificent with its cobblestone streets and ancient statues.

I later learned that he had a large *Reader's Digest* map book with him in the van, essentially a tourist guide with photos and information about every part of Canada. While his primary focus was his run, he was, in fact, touring the country and interested in everything he saw. I think that's why he would always backtrack when it came time to stop for food or take a break. He was adamant that he did not want to see what was ahead of him; he wanted to experience everything firsthand as he ran.

He also made good progress in Quebec, until the winds picked up. Terry could run in rain and snow and blazing heat but wind was particularly difficult for him. In Canada, the prevailing winds are almost always from the west, meaning that they were against him for most of his journey. They were so strong in parts of Quebec that he could barely move. The guys figured out how to use the van as a windshield, with Darrell sitting in the back holding one of its doors open and Terry running close behind. Doug would try to drive at Terry's pace with Darrell giving him instructions to speed up or slow down. It helped, but the exhaust fumes made Terry nauseous and Darrell had to watch his brother struggle for hours on end.

"I'd look into Terry's eyes," said Darrell. "It was like he was looking at nothing, like he was chasing the van, like he was going to hop on for a ride. It hurt having to watch him suffering. He'd run by a pole and I'd watch it get farther and farther away, then another would take its place. He wouldn't look at me so I'd watch his face a lot. He had to wear a jacket, the wind was blowing so hard. I watched it blowing his curls back from his face."

He had his picture taken with Gérard Côté, the four-time winner of the Boston Marathon, in Quebec City and the newspaper *Le Soleil* put him on its front page. Otherwise, he'd been running anonymously in the province. The only people who seemed to recognize him or know what he was doing were people with out-of-province license plates, particularly truckers for Home Hardware. Drivers for the Kitchener-based retail chain had all somehow heard about the Marathon of Hope and honked their horns in recognition. This little gesture of support from one company buoyed Terry's spirits and gave him faith that his story was gaining traction, at least in Ontario. Quebeckers were friendly enough but when they stopped on the highway, it was usually to offer him a lift. In one hundred mile stretch of running, he raised only $35.

It was simply a matter of awareness and the reluctance of the Quebec division of the Canadian Cancer Society to support the Marathon of Hope. This would change over time. Quebec today is a leading fundraiser for the Terry Fox Foundation. When Quebec schools hold a Terry Fox Run, they raise more money per student than anywhere else in Canada and, last I looked, of the fifteen streets named for Terry in Canada, ten are in Quebec. Some people in the province have been inspired to commit to their own marathons, including cancer survivor Les Hay who by the age of seventy-five had raised $500,000 for cancer research over forty-two years. But while Terry was there, it was mostly frustration for him.

Ray and I did what we could for Terry, Doug, and Darrell while we were with him in Quebec. We drove back and forth picking up supplies, finding a quiet location for his noon break, and searching out a motel for the evening. I was determined that they weren't going to spend another night in that cramped, smelly van. It must have been unhealthy as well as uncomfortable.

Travelling with him on those busy Quebec roads also impressed upon me the need to take extra precautions when he hit the even busier highways in Ontario. We would have a police escort and I would be accompanying him in my car, possibly along with others. I called the great Deborah Kirk and had her order a large sign that would attach to a car roof and read "Slow—Runner Ahead." The idea was that it could be mounted to a vehicle that would drop back a safe distance from Terry and warn them of what was up ahead. It would become a regular part of his entourage just after Ottawa.

On June 20, we ended the day west of St. Hyacinth. The three young men stayed at a rural convent on the beautiful Yamaska River, each in his own sparsely furnished cell, which was at least warm and dry. Ray and I drove ahead to Montreal and checked into the palatial Four Seasons courtesy of Izzy Sharp, owner of the chain. Izzy was a business partner with Eddie Creed who, as I mentioned, was part of our Toronto organizing committee, but they had each come aboard separately.

Izzy, in fact, felt a special bond with the Fox family. He had lost his son, Chris, to cancer. He identified with Betty and Rolly. "I knew what they were going through, the sense of hopelessness that comes with this dreaded disease. There is no feeling more difficult to deal with than that, and talking to Betty Fox, I could hear the pain in her voice." Izzy offered Terry and crew free rooms, wherever he had a hotel along our route for the duration of the run. It was a godsend.

The Four Seasons was a treat but we couldn't linger the next morning. Terry was approaching the Jacques Cartier Bridge which would bring him into Montreal. It seemed like the whole world was there that weekend. The Canadian Open golf tournament was at the Royal Montreal Golf Club. Olympic Stadium was filled to capacity for a boxing match between champions Sugar Ray Leonard and Roberto Duran. It was also the St.-Jean Baptiste holiday weekend. There were crowds on every corner. Montreal was one big party.

About the only place you couldn't find a crowd was on René Lévesque Boulevard, the route Terry took into the centre of the city, heading towards the Four Seasons Hotel. We'd been met at the far end of the bridge by a handful of runners who joined Terry, theoretically to collect donations, but there was no one to collect from. It was soul crushing.

Closer to our destination, in a nice surprise, we were joined by several wheelchair athletes and Don Sweet, an all-star for the Montreal Alouette football team, the first of many professional sports stars Terry would meet on the run. As usual, Terry turned on his jets when people ran with him, impressing upon him that the Marathon of Hope was no walk in the park.

A radio station vehicle was following us for the first time in the run, at least to my knowledge. It was CJAD, the sister station to CKFM back in Toronto. It was reporting live to listeners in both the Montreal and Toronto markets. Our new friends in Toronto were doing their part.

We were given a great reception at the Four Seasons. Bev Norris, the head of public relations for the hotel chain, had pulled out all stops. There was a half decent crowd and an array of media people. Renowned Toronto boxing manager and promoter Irv Ungerman showed up with a big stogie hanging out of his mouth, dressed to the nines. He handed Terry a crisp $100 bill, more than he had raised in several days.

Pictures of Terry from these events show him with a big smile. He was learning how to work the media. Later, however, he told me how disappointed he was with everything that had happened outside the hotel. He'd finally made it to one of Canada's largest cities and he'd hardly made a dent. I smiled and told him, "Just consider it a rehearsal, big changes are ahead."

After the reception, Terry headed up to his room for a rest. He had his own suite. Doug and Darrell were sharing, as were Ray and I. Compared to how they'd been living on the road, the guys felt like they'd landed on another planet. Ray and I hung out in Doug and Darrell's room. With his usual sense of fun, Darrell checked out the minibar and decided to give Courvoisier a try.

There he was, stretched out on the floor, wee bottle in hand, watching the Roadrunner cartoons on TV. Intermittently, the set would turn fuzzy and the picture would jump. Darrell would slap the side of the TV to correct the glitch. Bev Norris happened by the room and noticed this behaviour.

"Do you realize that this is a $500-a-night room?" she asked in mock seriousness.

"What would it cost if the TV worked?" said Darrell, not missing a beat.

He got a laugh out of Bev. We all appreciated Darrell's humour. He was a great foil to his brother and Doug and kept things from getting too heavy at any moment.

Re-energized by his nap, Terry ate lunch and headed back out to finish his run, touching the exact light standard he had finished at earlier in the day. No short cuts.

Seeing how he handled the public at the Four Seasons reception, how he rolled with the disappointing turnouts in yet another province but remained resolutely committed to the discipline of his run, I was in awe of him all over again.

I drove him back to the hotel in my car at the end of the day. We were chatting about how things were going and I was feeling overwhelmed by wonder and admiration for him. Even though I wasn't travelling with him day in and day out, he was consuming my every waking minute. During a moment as we drove, without looking at him and without really thinking about it, I said: "I don't know if you will understand this, but I love you."

I don't know where it came from but it just had to be said.

He smiled and said: "I understand."

My feelings about Terry hadn't come out of nowhere. They probably reflected where I was at that moment in my life. The truth was that I needed that job with the Canadian Cancer Society and I needed an inspiration like Terry Fox.

My life had fallen apart in 1979. It was nothing as dire as a cancer diagnosis and an amputation but it felt like I'd lost everything. After a string of career successes as a radio reporter, city alderman, and chamber of commerce manager, I'd invested my life savings in a Radio Shack franchise in Welland.

It bankrupted me. I had a wife, Chris, and two children, Kerry Anne, nine, and Patrick, eight. Suddenly we were broke. We lost the house and the car. Or, rather, I lost the house and the car. It was me who messed up.

I started selling life insurance to make ends meet and I wasn't very good at it. I can't describe the dark feelings of depression crushing me at that time.

One evening I chastised Kerry Anne for having holes in her socks. Then I saw there were holes in the bottoms of her shoes. I asked why she didn't tell me.

"Because I know we don't have any money," she said.

I cried. What would you do? I was a complete failure. I couldn't support myself, let alone my family.

In December 1979, I heard about a job with the Canadian Cancer Society in London, Ontario, my wife's home town. They were looking for a district director. I had been a volunteer for several years, as well as with the Kiwanis and the United Way. I applied, thinking I had a good shot at it.

I drove from Welland to London for the interview. By the time I got home, they'd called to say I had the job. Elation. I thought I might just be able to save my marriage. I might be able to pull myself up from the depths of depression, too.

The next morning, I got another call. They had changed their minds. A board member was retiring and they had decided to give him the position. Needless to say, I was devastated. I'd gone from zero to hero and back again in the space of twelve hours. I later learned that the real reason I was rejected was that someone in the London chapter had learned that as a twelve-year-old I'd nearly burned down a school.

It was true. I grew up in St. Thomas, Ontario and I liked to go to the movies. One week in 1955, I saw Audie Murphy in *To Hell and Back* at the Roxy Theatre. Murphy was a pint-sized fireball, a genuine decorated World War 2 combat veteran who played himself on the big screen. He made a big impression on me, a kid who spent every weekend playing "war" down the street from our three-storey red brick house on Flora Street. We were less than a decade removed from the war and it loomed large in our consciousness.

Two years later, I inherited a paper route from my older brothers, delivering the *St. Thomas Times Journal*. I hated it. The papers would arrive at 4 p.m. I had to fold them and head across the street to the Arthur Voaden Technical School (later a secondary school), the first stop on my route, up three flights of stairs to the library. It was an awful way to start and I would often waste time pretending I was Audie Murphy, dodging through the bushes, fighting imaginary Nazis, instead of lugging the papers. Customers would complain, particularly grumpy old Mr. Sutherland who lived on the corner. He would call my parents: "Bill is in the bushes across the street and I have been waiting an hour for my paper!"

One day I was especially caught up in my imaginary battles. I'd just dropped the paper at the library when I came under surprise attack from a Nazi company. Using a rolled-up paper as a machine gun, I fought them off as I backed myself down the hallway. Running out of imaginary bullets, I used my imaginary supply of grenades. Then it was down to hand-to-hand combat. Reaching the bottom of the stairs, I decided to set up a smoke screen. It was something Audie would do.

I lit fire to a piece of paper hanging on an old cork bulletin board. Whoosh! The whole board burst into flames. I panicked, ran out the side door, down an alley, and waited to see smoke in the sky and hear the sirens.

As it happened, the student council president noticed the burning bulletins, grabbed a fire extinguisher, and saved the school, not to mention my ass.

The next morning, I'm at school—Grade Six at Holy Angels. I get a message that Father White wants to see me in his office. Uh oh.

I know it's bad. I walk through the door and find Father White with a very grim look on his face, sitting with two detectives in suits and ties and fedoras.

I confessed immediately. They asked me to sign a statement. Father White steps in and says no one signs anything until my parents arrive after school. That gave me time to plan my getaway.

I ran home at lunch time, collected the paper route money my mother had saved for me, and ran away from home. My plan was to hitchhike to Windsor, maybe cross the frozen Detroit River. From there, who knew? Florida, perhaps, and on to Cuba. I made it as far as Blenheim, a distance of fifty miles. I stopped there at a small restaurant and ordered a burger and fries. A very large policeman plopped himself down next to me. He knew I was up to something.

Long story short, a phone call was made, my parents picked me up, my mother cried all the way home, my father literally kicked my ass. In subsequent weeks, I visited the Ontario Psychiatric Hospital where I was diagnosed as a normal twelve-year-old boy with a very fertile imagination. I quit the paper route. Otherwise, life went on.

The whole episode receded into the past but was not entirely forgotten. The people who had hired me for the job at the district office in London had called around to their subsidiary offices, including the one in St. Thomas, where to my great misfortune someone recalled the legend of Bill Vigars and the flaming bulletin board. "You can't hire that guy," they said. "He tried to burn down a school."

It was a bleak Christmas at our house. It made Dickens' A Christmas Carol seem a comedy by comparison. The New Year started with me in complete despair.

As the volunteer chair of the Canadian Cancer Society's public relations committee in Welland, I attended the society's annual conference in Toronto that month. I heard about a much bigger job: the Ontario division was hiring a province-wide public relations and fundraising lead. I contacted Harry Rowlands who, again, was the provincial executive director. He said the interviews were finished but if I could get him my resume, he'd see what he could do. I made the ninety-minute trip back to Welland, picked up my resume, and drove all the way back to Toronto.

I was interviewed by Harry as well as Ron Potter and Ron Calhoun who, again, were the volunteer chairs of the public relations and fundraising committees for Ontario and Canada, respectively. Ron Calhoun, the guy who had come up with the Marathon of Hope, urged Harry to sign me up: "Hire this guy. He thinks outside the box." He wasn't wrong. It's just the way I am. Half the time, I'm not aware the box exists. I may not be detail-oriented or much of an administrator, but I like trying new things and I've never been afraid to ask anyone for anything—what's the worst they can say? No?

Fortunately, no one ever said anything about a flaming bulletin board from twenty-three years earlier when I was an (admittedly mischievous) kid. The fact that someone in St. Thomas had used it against me when I applied for the lesser job in London turned out to be a fantastic break. Harry hired me. Being a director of public relations and fundraising at the provincial level was a much better job than being a director of the same at the district level.

More importantly, I may never have spent any time with Terry Fox in the lesser role and I certainly wouldn't have been in a position to do much for him or the Marathon of Hope.

While I was hugely relieved to be gainfully employed, it wasn't all good news. I had to move to Toronto. By then, there was little hope of saving my marriage. I'd have to get a new place—I'd never lived alone before—and see my kids on weekends. The whole process was bruising. But at least I would be able to provide for my family.

By the time Terry was in Quebec, I'd settled into an apartment in Thorncliffe Park, overlooking the Don Valley Parkway. We were developing a new family routine. Every Friday night, I would pick up the kids from Welland and bring them back to the apartment for the weekend. Chris, who had recently graduated from Niagara College, found a job as a social worker.

We were getting by and I was gradually climbing out of the emotional black hole I'd been in for months. But I really needed my new job to work. I was desperate to make an impression—to make a difference. And maybe more than I realized at the time, I was looking for some kind of spark. In Terry, I'd found a shooting star.

CHAPTER SEVEN

Footballs and Politicians

IN THEIR VERY EARLY CONVERSATIONS before Terry started his run, Ron Calhoun had advised him not to take the most direct route across Canada. He could have run from Montreal to Ottawa and straight across Northern Ontario to Thunder Bay and saved himself a lot of mileage but he would have missed Southern Ontario, the most densely populated part of the country, and Toronto, where most of our national broadcasters and big media companies are located.

When I had first talked to Terry over the telephone from Nova Scotia, we had worked out a plan that would have him arrive in Ottawa on Canada Day, July 1. There would be big crowds and a lot of media—it was an opportunity to make a splash. We solidified this plan when we met in person in Edmundston and had him arriving in Toronto on July 11.

He was on schedule when he hit Montreal. In fact, he was a day ahead of schedule. I was annoyed to read in a Toronto newspaper that "Bill Vigars and the Canadian Cancer Society made Terry take a day off in Montreal." For starters, it was impossible to get Terry to do something he didn't want to do. It was his run and his was always the last word. The Canadian Cancer Society, moreover, had no clue what decisions were being made on the road. The reason Terry took the day off in Montreal was simply because Terry had arrived in Montreal one day early and we wanted to be in Ottawa for Canada Day.

I thought Terry would be energized by the brief pause, maybe enjoy himself a little and rejuvenate his body. I was wrong. He wasn't at all happy about the break. It interrupted his momentum. He tried to relax, attending the Canadian Open Golf Tournament with Doug, Darrell, and a friend from high school, Clay Gamble, but he was relieved to get back on the road, dodging urban traffic, the next morning, never mind that the temperature was in the thirties.

Ray and I stayed with the run until Lachute, a day out of Ottawa. I joined the guys for a dip in the motel pool before heading for Toronto where I had to clean up some paperwork and brief Harry Rowlands on how things were progressing. I had impressed upon Harry and Ron Potter how important it was for them to be on hand when Terry crossed into Ontario and, to their credit, they needed no coaxing.

From Toronto, I headed to Welland to pick up my kids, who had just started their summer vacations. I'd asked Terry if it was okay for them to join us along the route. He agreed. Terry was great with kids and would form a strong bond with them over the weeks to come.

All of our attention was now riveted on making sure the receptions in Ottawa went off with a bang. We were fortunate that two men mentioned previously, volunteer Major Terry Christopher and Ottawa district director Jack Hillard, had started organizing even before the Ontario division of the Canadian Cancer Society had decided to throw its weight behind the Marathon of Hope.

Major Christopher had started one of the earliest breast cancer screening programs in the Canadian military when he was stationed at Camp Borden. That caught the eye of the Canadian Cancer Society's office in Toronto. Subsequently posted at National Defence Headquarters in Ottawa, he developed the first second-career assistance network for retiring military personnel. In short, he was a leader, someone who could get things done. Jack Hilliard, who apart from being a retired artillery officer in the Canadian Armed Forces, was the society's district director for Eastern Ontario. They were a great team.

Major Christopher had been part of that urgent meeting in Toronto where a commitment was finally made to back Terry. He and Hilliard couldn't understand why their counterparts in other districts weren't interested in helping out. They sensed a lot of politics in the room as well as a simple reluctance to put in extra effort. On their drive home, they determined that they would be largely on their own when Terry showed up in their district and that they'd better get ready. I took those two strong military minds and some good old Canadian Armed Forces grit and determination to see things through.

The two men split up responsibilities, enlisted local service clubs as well as business and political leaders, to generate support and a sense of excitement. They wanted to make it absolutely clear to Terry things would change from the moment he crossed the Ottawa River.

Terry crossed the river at Hawkesbury with Doug and Darrell, entirely unobserved, at 5 a.m. on June 28. The town was sound asleep and Terry wanted to get his morning nine miles accomplished before driving back to where he'd stopped the night before and making his official crossing timed for a celebratory reception. Jumping back and forth like this on occasion allowed Terry to meet his public and still chalk up mileage.

Around noon, he started across the Perley Bridge from Grenville Quebec—his ceremonial entrance to Ontario. On the Hawkesbury side, a high school band banged out a rousing version of "Georgie Girl." Why they picked that tune I'll never know but it was their enthusiasm that counted. Balloons were released into the sky. A crowd of local dignitaries met Terry in front of the community center along with PeeWee baseball players, families and kids—lots of kids.

Terry made a speech thanking the Canadian Cancer Society and the community. He took the time to meet people individually, especially the kids, who asked him about the run and his prosthesis. After about fifteen minutes, he said his goodbyes and with a big smile and a wave, jumped into the van and headed back to the exact spot where he had finished off that morning. He still had seventeen miles to run that day.

My kids and I had arrived in Ottawa that afternoon and checked into the Four Seasons, a treat for all of us. We headed down to the pool. This is my son Pat's recollection of what happened next:

> Kerry and I were taking turns jumping off dad's shoulders. After my turn, I was coming up from under the water, about to reach the edge and I saw a pair of blue Adidas shoes. I was shocked and shy at first meeting Terry. He had just came back from running and I remember how his hair was wet from sweat, but mostly I remember his big smile and him asking if I was having a good time. He was really friendly and I liked him right away. Later, up in his room, Dad said: 'Show the kids how your leg works.' He moved his real leg up and down a few times and said 'See, just like yours.' I remember he was very friendly and he was really funny.

The leg joke was one of our standards on the road. It worked every time. I had brought with me new t-shirts for the team, this time with Darrell's name spelled right. The kids had theirs, too, so that police and organizers in each town would know they were part of the team and that it was okay for them to be around. They were up early the next morning and joined in Terry's routine, running beside him for spells and getting his water and oranges ready.

Entering Ottawa along Sussex Drive, we were told that we should make a detour to a reception at Rideau Hall, the governor general's official residence. We ran up the long drive and entered the marble-floored foyer of the residence, feeling completely underdressed in our running outfits. We had arrived in the middle of another reception for the crisply dressed winners of *Reach for the Top*, the long-running CBC television show featuring brilliant high school students competing to prove who knew the most. They were gracious about our intervention.

We were all handed crystal stemmed glasses with orange bubbly, refreshing after the morning run. In the middle of a very quiet moment, Darrell, much to his embarrassment, accidentally dropped his glass, shattering it on the floor. Governor General Ed Schreyer made light of it and turned what might have been an awkward situation into a humorous one.

After our brief toast, we were back on the road, heading to downtown Ottawa. Terry had never been to Ottawa before yet was sufficiently aware of his surroundings to spot the War Memorial when turning at the Chateau Laurier Hotel towards the Sparks Street Mall. What he did next was remarkable: rather than simply running across the War Memorial square, he made a hard right turn and ran all the way around it as a sign of respect. It was another moment for me to be genuinely impressed by this young man.

The mall was packed: a massive crowd of people waiting just for Terry. There were so many bodies that he had to weave from side to side in order to make his way to a stage that Major Christopher and Jack Hilliard had arranged to have set up in the middle of the mall. There were cheers and rousing applause. Terry was deeply moved and gave a longer, heartfelt speech about his cause and his memories of seeing children in the cancer ward back home. He asked people to dig deep for their donations to fund the cancer research he so ardently believed was needed. The response was overwhelming. It lifted Terry emotionally and psychologically. He felt that his message was finally breaking through.

Afterward we all headed back to the Four Seasons where Bev Norris had organized a first-class VIP reception. There were more helium balloons released from the rooftop—helium balloons were a big thing back then. Harry and Ron represented the Canadian Cancer Society and the federal minister of transport, Jean Luc Pepin, represented the federal government.

Notwithstanding the dignitaries, the stars of the reception, apart from Terry, were two young men from the Kingston area, Garth Walker and Jim Brown. They were the first two individuals to visit the society's Toronto office to ask permission to fundraise for Terry. I'll let Jim tell their story and what he recalls of that day:

Garth and I happened to be on a ten-day bike ride from Kingston up through Ottawa to Mount Tremblant and back. As we left Montreal, Garth had spotted a Terry Fox poster in the Four Seasons Hotel. Terry was not yet in the public consciousness but Garth hatched the idea of doing a fund-raising ride in a few weeks from Toronto to Ottawa in twenty-four hours. We both loved to ride and were in top shape. We committed to do it as we rode back to Kingston.

Garth's aunt Shirley, whose family owns Hawkins Cheezies, the famous brand of genuine cheezies, was a big supporter of the Canadian Cancer Society in Belleville. He phoned her at some point and got a big positive response. Next thing I recall we were pitching the idea to Bill Vigars at the Canadian Cancer Society.

It was about four or five weeks before Terry was to arrive in Ottawa. Immediately, we began a blitz of cold calls from Toronto to Ottawa, pestering any and all media who would listen to promote our ride. Garth was a cold-call master. We did a lot of talking.

My brothers and partners at Browns, our family-owned company, agreed to cover for me while I worked on this project and loaned us a company van that we plastered with Terry Fox posters. We brought in our circle of family and friends and enlisted them to spread the word.

With Garths parents and friends, we held a Terry Fox promotional rally at Nathan Phillips Square in Toronto the day before our ride. Hundreds of signatures with good wishes and pledges were gathered to present to Terry.

We rode out at sunrise the next morning. Coming into Belleville there was a torrential rainstorm, at times making it almost impossible to see. Shirley had arranged for us to stop and greet local cancer supporters in Bellville as well as the mayor. It was a brief visit and some welcome nourishment, and we were off again.

We rode over a lot of hills that night. Sometimes we were riding by flashlight, with our support crew yelling at us so we wouldn't fall asleep on the bikes. When the sun came up we got revitalized. Finally, we arrived at Sparks Street and met Terry and the team on the hotel roof. We presented our signatures and pledges. It was wonderful to see so many people were cheering him along by this time. That evening, we had dinner with Terry and some local supporters including Ron Fox, a giant of a man who played linebacker for the Ottawa Rough Riders.

After a few hours of much needed sleep, we got up at 4 a.m. and ran with Terry that day along Highway 7. At one point, his artificial joint was jamming so we used WD-40 from our bike kit to get it working properly.

For my part, I can tell you it was the best of real life. It was exhausting and emotional, complete with sobbing in a hotel room. It was exhilarating and uplifting to be around this young man with such a big heart as he gave everything he had to the world. It was humbling in a very good way that has lasted a lifetime. Terry is amongst the angels in my heart and mind, as he is with so many others.

I was in the lobby of the hotel that day when Richard Getz, publicity manager for the Ottawa Rough Riders (now the Red Blacks), walked up to me. Richard had a problem. His team was playing the Saskatchewan Roughriders in a rare pre-season afternoon game the next day—Canada Day. Governor General Schreyer's office had called to inform the team that he would not be able to perform the ceremonial opening kick-off as planned. Richard was stuck. On his way to the Four Seasons—he had been invited to represent the Ottawa Rough Riders at the reception—he'd come up with a solution. He asked if Terry would do the ceremonial kick off the next day.

Until that moment, our plan for Canada Day—not much of a plan, in retrospect—had been to crash the ceremonies on Parliament Hill and see if we could get Terry recognized on the CBC live broadcast. I told Richard I would talk to Terry after his nap and relay the offer. When we discussed the matter, Terry's immediate reaction was "I'd rather go to a football game." A wise decision, as it turned out. I called Richard to let him know it was a go.

As Richard recalls:

Game days at Landsdowne Park were always exciting, but there was an electricity in the air that day suggesting it was not going to be just another pre-season game.

Terry and his team arrived close to an hour before game time because Terry wanted to practice kicking. He wanted it to go well.

Unfortunately, the security guards had no idea who Terry was and made Doug park the van a fair distance from the stadium.

I grabbed some balls and a tee and Terry and Bill Vigars and I went into the empty Civic Centre arena, lit by a single ceiling light and the exit signs. Under the north side stands, Terry practiced on the concrete floor for a good half hour. He was having second thoughts, worried that he might fall or shank the ball, but decided to go through with it.

The time came and Terry was introduced by Rough Rider public-address announcer Bob LaBelle. As he walked out of the tunnel onto the field, the crowd of 17,000 erupted into a thundering standing ovation.

With both teams lined up at centre field, Terry was greeted by future CFL Hall of Fame tight end, Tony Gabriel, and Rough

Rider all-time leading scorer Gerry Organ in preparation for the ceremonial kick.

I've since talked to Gerry and he vividly remembers Terry's excitement and his nervousness but, more than anything, his determination. He knew what the moment meant to the Marathon of Hope and he was going to do this to the best of his ability, just like everything else he was doing.

Gerry set the ball on the tee and moments later Terry launched a decent kick to the awaiting Saskatchewan players who promptly returned it to him to commemorate the event.

Gabriel and Organ presented him with a ball autographed by the entire team as well as an Ottawa team jersey. Terry looked at Organ and said he wished he could have done better. Organ told him there wasn't anyone in the CFL who could do what he was doing, which brought a smile to Terry's face. As he left the field, the crowd stood and cheered wildly again.

That event and the aftermath had a profound effect on everyone but probably nobody more than Tony Gabriel, whose father, John, had died of cancer at the age of fifty-seven. Since his retirement, Tony has helped organize Terry Fox runs back in his home town of Burlington.

My own father, Wil, was sixty-one-years-old and terminally ill with abdominal cancer at the time. He was also deeply moved by Terry and went on to be a volunteer board member of the Ottawa West Cancer Society not long after. My Dad was so proud of Terry and lived his own plight, day by day, vicariously through Terry's battle with cancer.

For the record, the score that day was 29-3 in favour of Ottawa, but the clear winners were Terry Fox and the Marathon of Hope.

It was a great day but Terry's schedule left no room for celebrations. We were on the move as day broke the next morning, driving out to the spot he had finished at the day before. Just after noon, Major Christopher and Jack Hilliard showed up to take us to Parliament Hill. We were about to cross a big item off Terry's wish list: meeting the prime minister.

We pulled up at the Parliament buildings and waited for Pierre Trudeau on a landing near his office. We were all there, including Doug, Darrell, and my kids, who sat on their haunches at Terry's feet. Terry was going to ask Trudeau to run with him in the Ottawa area. We hoped, at least, that the meeting would boost Terry's visibility and fund-raising efforts.

The prime minister finally emerged from the House of Commons, unfortunately in a foul temper. He'd just been battered by the opposition in Question Period. He was in no mood for a meet-and-greet and didn't know who Terry was or what he was doing, let alone why. He had not been briefed by his staff. It was awkward and embarrassing.

In the middle of the stilted conversation, Trudeau suddenly looked down and the kids and asked, "And who are you?"

They both jumped up and shook his hand and took over the conversation, enthusiastically explaining Terry's journeys as the photographers took pictures of the four of them. The picture appeared in the papers the next day and the kids still have copies—mementos of the time as grade-schoolers that they'd managed to break the ice at an historic meeting.

Trudeau never did run with Terry. It was a missed opportunity for both of them, although having a picture with the prime minister did give a boost to the Marathon of Hope. Terry had no bad feelings about the encounter. That wasn't in his nature. He just kept looking ahead, eager to get back on the highway.

CHAPTER EIGHT

Big Jack Sees Something

THE COUNTRY-SINGER WILLIE NELSON HAD a hit song 1980, *On the Road Again,* and it was ringing in my ears every day as we rolled through Eastern Ontario. I liked to think Willie was thinking of us when he wrote it. Those were perfect summer days, warm and clear, although it could get a bit oppressive for Terry running in the heat and humidity. He soldiered on, one telephone pole at a time. That was how he counted the distance. Each pole was a marker. He didn't dwell on the twenty-six miles he needed to cover that day: just the next pole, then the next one, and so on.

We'd said goodbye to our Ottawa friends and now joined up with "Big Jack" Lambert, as Terry called him. He would accompany us all the way down Highway 7 to Oshawa. He was a jovial, gentle, and he knew the territory well. He had contacts in every community we passed through and was able to supplement the advance work I had done along the route with his own arrangements. Terry was very fond of Big Jack.

We were on a two-lane highway again but now were accompanied by the red flashing lights of an Ontario Provincial Police cruiser, with Jack trailing in his own car, fifty yards behind. He'd had a sign made for the car roof that said "Slow—Runner Ahead" on one side and "Donations Accepted Here" on the other. The convoy left us all feeling better about Terry's safety.

At 5 a.m. on the second morning out of Ottawa, the van pulled up at the spot that Terry had reached the day before. It was still dark. I was with the kids in a separate car. A black-and-white cruiser was sitting on the gravel shoulder of the road, waiting for us.

I had been told by Jim Butticci, a retired spokesperson for the OPP, that the assignment of accompanying the run would be given to new recruits or soon-to-retire desk jockeys. It wasn't a glamorous assignment, driving all day at four miles per hour directly behind a one-legged runner.

Knowing this, I immediately headed to the police cruiser to identify myself and thank the officer for being there. It was a routine I would repeat every morning.

I quickly got the sense that the officer was not too enthused with his assignment. I wasn't sure if he'd just come on duty or had been a last-minute replacement or what but it seemed something was amiss. There was no mistaking his gruffness and "why am I here?" attitude. I wasn't entirely unsympathetic. Who wants to be at work at 5 a.m.? Even I wasn't used to it yet.

"Okay everyone, let's move," I said and Terry ran two miles before taking his first break.

As we pulled over on to the shoulder, the van crew readied Terry's water while I walked up to the driver's side of the police car to see if everything was okay. The officer was staring at Terry, who was standing by the van. I noticed a tear running down the officer's face. He turned and looked at me. "I have never seen anything like this, ever," he said. "How is he doing that?"

The officer's transformation was something I witnessed daily with Terry. I didn't have an answer to that question, no matter how many times I heard it.

Later that morning, the sun was shining and traffic had picked up. Cars, motorhomes, and pickups would slow down to say hello. Many would pull over to the side of the road ahead of us and someone would jump out to take a picture or hand the crew a donation. Vehicles travelling in the opposite direction would do the same.

I noticed that some people were pulling up or running to the police cruiser, trying to give the officer donations. "I can't be doing that," he told me. He was on duty.

I smiled at his plight and shrugged my shoulders as if to say, "I can't stop them."

He surrendered and for the rest of his shift held his arm out the driver's side window, cap in hand accepting donations from passing cars.

I am sure that officer prizes the photo he had taken with Terry at the end of the day. I know I'll never forget his reaction. It was typical of how quickly Terry made converts to his cause. At its simplest, the Marathon of Hope was a fundraiser and a way to raise awareness about cancer. What most of us would only appreciate in time was that it became much more. Terry put a human face on cancer. He brought it home to every person he met—everyone who saw him out there on the road, literally fighting the disease.

The response on the road that day was heartening. All the people stopping, waving, honking. Terry even waylaid a Toronto to Ottawa bus that day, the Voyageur line, if I remember correctly. It pulled over to the south shoulder about a half mile ahead of Terry. As he ran towards it, the bus emptied and the passengers lined up on the side of the road, cheering and applauding. As I approached the driver, he handed me a wad of cash that a passenger had collected. It was a special moment and more evidence of Terry's magic.

On July 4, with the temperature nearing thirty degrees, we arrived at the first of the small towns I had visited weeks before. Kaladar was perched at the junction of Highway 7 and Highway 41, 100 miles west of Ottawa. It was the town where a volunteer named Glenda Bence had told me, "If he makes it this far, we'll do something." I felt Kaladar was a test of whether Ottawa had been a fluke or we had generated real community support.

Terry ended the day just east of the town and, as usual, went backward to a motel for the night. The next morning, he started his run through town arriving just after 5 a.m. The roadway was already lined with people standing in the dark to give Terry an enthusiastic welcome. I swear the entire town came out to greet and cheer him on.

After reaching Terry's twelve-mile point, we came back to town for his morning nap at a local motel but before retiring spent some time talking to Glenda. She was the matriarch of the family that owned the local car dealership—a warm personality with a huge smile. She was surrounded by a gaggle of kids who told Terry they were off to a bike-a-thon to raise funds for him. Glenda, who had not been on a bike for years, was going to join them.

When he got up from his nap, Terry made a point of staying in Kaladar until the bike-a-thoners returned, particularly Glenda. He joked that he was concerned she might hurt herself. They had a good laugh and on we went. Two decades later, Glenda and the community would unveil a plaque in honour of the twentieth anniversary of Terry's visit. "He was a wonderful boy and we all felt that he had just walked into our hearts," said Glenda, choking back tears at the memory.

I could tell a story like that for every town we visited that summer.

Terry seemed at times to be floating on air due to the reception and support he was getting. And it grew every day. The only problems were the heat and humidity. And then, around Peterborough, the dreaded wind picked up. This was the first time I'd personally seen Terry struggle against the wind. It was hard to watch. Doug and Darrell reverted to the method they had used before, opening the back doors of the van with Darrell sitting over the bumper, facing Terry, as Doug tried to drive at Terry's pace. Again, it helped but created another problem: the exhaust from the van was blowing in Terry's face.

I thought there had to be a solution to the exhaust problem. That morning, Terry took his usual post-breakfast nap a roadside, single-storey motel/restaurant. The police contingent and several members of the public lingered in the parking lot. As usual everyone had been asked to be quiet so as not to disturb Terry. I headed down the road to the first garage I came across and explained the situation to the owner. He as on it in a flash, grabbing a long piece of black hose he used to vent exhaust out of the garage bay while working on vehicles. He jumped in his truck and followed me back to the motel.

This guy was a genius. He had brought a roll of chicken wire to secure one end of the hose to the exhaust pipe. He then ran the hose up the van's rear ladder, wiring it to the individual rungs. He handed the far end of the hose up to Doug, who was on the roof, ready to wire it to the top rack.

Doug thought it might be a good idea to test the contraption. He instructed Darrell to climb into the driver's seat. While looking into the hose, Doug yelled to Darrell: "Turn it on."

Darrell turned on the ignition and floored it. Whoosh! The contents of the well-used hose shot out, turning Doug's face completely black. We all erupted in laughter. Terry's motel room door flung open—he was about to give us heck for disturbing him but took one look at Doug and doubled over in laughter.

As luck would have it, the wind had died by the time Terry was ready to run again. Nevertheless, the hose remained on the van for much of the rest of the run.

Peterborough gave Terry a tremendous reception. He spoke at a lunch-hour service club meeting, the room so quiet you could have heard the proverbial pin drop.

As a measure of the growing profile of the Marathon of Hope, we confronted a new problem in Peterborough. I had to intervene in conversations between local police and the always present OPP. As a matter of pride, the local constabulary insisted on escorting Terry. The OPP felt the assignment was its own. I negotiated a detente between the forces. The OPP would escort Terry to the edge of town. There, the local force would take over. The provincial officers would still be part of the convoy, dropping to the rear of the line until we exited town, at which point they would retake the lead position. It was an improvised arrangement acceptable to all and we would arrange to do the same in advance of reaching other towns along the route.

After a night's rest in Peterborough, we started down Route 115, which would be our last stretch of rural highway for a while. We were only a few days out from Toronto, which we'd approach down Highway 2.

By this time, the heat and humidity were wearing on Terry. At one of his rest breaks, he came to me to say that he was running out of a special cream created for him before he had left BC. It helped with the chaffing of the skin on his stump. He was in a great deal of pain. He showed me what he was enduring. It was not pretty.

Big Jack had arranged for Terry to take his afternoon break at a Canadian Cancer Society volunteer's home situated on a large farm.

It was a beautiful two-storey, red brick house with a wide, wrap-around white veranda. Three large oak trees shaded the exterior. As Terry napped, the rest of the team—Darrell, Doug, Big Jack, and a policeman—lounged outside on chairs and around a picnic table. A slight breeze broke the heat. The air buzzed with the sound of cicadas. I remembered it well. The summer song of cicadas was a constant in my rural Ontario childhood.

While we were stopped, I called my brother, Bob, a professor of kinesiology at the University of Western Ontario, where he worked with the men's and women's track and cross-country teams. I explained the situation. Bob called a contact in sports medicine at Queen's University, since they were closer. They were able to help with the cream but could not get anything to us for a couple of days.

After about four hours, Terry came out of the farmhouse looking refreshed and ready to go. We asked how he felt. He said the chaffing had cleared up. He still felt a little pain but he told us he'd washed it, applied some of the remaining cream, and it was okay.

Jack and I exchange a look of "how is this possible?"

Terry had amazing endurance and powers of recuperation. But I couldn't help but think back to a conversation I'd had with Jack a couple of nights before. It's stuck with me ever since. Terry had retired for the night. Darrell and Doug were off somewhere. I sat with Jack on rocking chairs on a cabin porch, overlooking a small lake. It was pure Canadiana.

In the middle of small talk about the day's events and the next day's plans, Jack said quietly: "There's something wrong with Terry. There's something he's not telling us."

It was a chilling statement. Jack couldn't pinpoint what it was, but he was quite emphatic.

I didn't see it and the conversation ended there. Jack never mentioned it again. But it haunted me, and it still does to this day. Did I miss something early on in the run? What if Jack was right? What if I'd had a straight talk with Terry? What if? What if?

The fact is that life is full of "what ifs" for all of us. We have to accept the past. But there would be more "what ifs" as the run progressed.

CHAPTER NINE

"Heck of a Way to Raise Money"

A S TERRY AND CREW HEADED west towards the Greater Toronto Area, I would slip back and forth to my downtown Toronto office at the Canadian Cancer Society. These short stints allowed me to check in with Deborah, but they were too short to catch any vibe about Terry and the run in the city. I wanted so badly to make a big splash in Toronto. I had to trust the people I'd met at the meeting in CKFM's boardroom: "Don't worry, we'll take care of things for Terry when he arrives." Fingers crossed.

Somewhere around Peterborough, I'd taken the kids back to Welland. Things were getting hectic for me and the kids had other things to do with their summer: Pat was missing soccer games and Kerry Anne wanted to spend some time with her friends and her Mom. The plan was for them to join with us again on the other side of Toronto.

I mentioned that Terry and Ron Calhoun had sketched out his route way back in winter. It had him running west from Toronto through Hamilton and along Highway 2 through Brantford, Woodstock and Thamesford as far as London. He then planned to turn back towards

Toronto along Highway 7 through St. Marys, Guelph and Kitchener before heading north. Terry had since told me he'd also like to run to Niagara Falls and Windsor. My response was incredulous: "When do you want to get home?"

I had to explain to him the distance from London to Windsor would add five days. Niagara Falls would add ten days more. Terry had become accustomed to looking at a roadmap where the distances can appear much shorter than the reality. He dropped that idea but I started the wheels rolling to somehow get him to Niagara Falls—again, part of Terry's motivation was to see the country and who can leave Ontario without seeing Niagara Falls?

The media was now picking up big time. I was regularly setting up phone interviews in the next town on our route to spread the word and make sure everyone knew when Terry would be running through. I'd often take Darrell with me to do the interviews. In between calls, I'd stay out on the road, running along with Darrell to collect donations from passing cars. There were so many people now and they all had money in their hands, often throwing it in the van window or in the Big Jack's front seat. At one point, we resorted to using a couple of green garbage bags to collect all the cash that was coming in. When I needed a rest, I'd jump on the fender of one of the escort vehicles. I was totally out of shape at the beginning of the run and Terry would tease me about my lack of athleticism. By the time we approached Toronto, I was getting almost thin from running in the constant heat.

Big Jack's granddaughter, fifteen-year-old Kim Langille (nee Wilson), came along for the ride. She'd been spending part of her summer vacation with her grandparents in Peterborough. Jack had come home at the end of one day and said to his wife, Muriel: "Kim has to come with me for the next couple of days. I have been with a young man who is going to make history." Muriel's reply in her soft Scot's burr was, "Oh Jack, I don't think that's a good idea for a young lady."

Jack was insistent and Kim joined the crew. I recently caught up with her over social media and she has vivid memories not only of the Terry and the run but of the down time, when she and Darrell would kick around a soccer ball, at one point surrounded by a very active flock of squawking chickens.

We checked into the Holiday Inn in Bowmanville just off the Highway 401 where Terry was warmly welcomed at a reception organized by local Canadian Cancer Society volunteers. After dinner, we headed to a nearby ballpark. A bantam baseball tournament was in progress and one of Kim's friends was playing. During the game, Darrell asked Jack if he could borrow his car to take Kim to Dairy Queen. Gentle Jack hands him the keys and off they go.

More than an hour later, they're still not back and Jack is getting concerned. This was his fifteen-year-old granddaughter, after all. The two finally returned to a gentle scolding. It would have been much sterner if we had realized that Darrell did not have a driver's license (he'd been sharing the driving since Nova Scotia). It's important to keep in mind that Darrell was just seventeen at the time, totally devoted to his brother, and that he brought a lot of companionship and a much-needed light touch to the crew and its daily challenges.

Bowmanville would be another big milestone in the Marathon of Hope but Terry did not sleep well that night. He'd run through a lot of heat and thunderstorms. The hotel had booked a large number of families and the kids seemed to spend the whole evening running up and down the hallways. Darrell, Doug, and I took turns sitting on the floor outside Terry's room, keeping the kids at bay until about 11 p.m. when, mercifully, they went to bed.

Terry rolled out of bed, as usual, at 4 a.m. to face another gruelling day with his usual dogged determination. The early mornings were a grind for him. It's not like he woke up every day, after having run a marathon the day before, and the day before that, and felt bright-eyed and refreshed.

That's why we were in awe of what he was doing. He just kept going and never complained, at least not about the task he'd undertaken.

I immediately sensed there was something different about this morning. It was 5 a.m. and there were already people standing on the roadside waiting for him. The sun wasn't close to being up. At one of his first water breaks, he stopped to say hello to a couple sitting in lawn chairs, coffee thermos nearby. They had been there since 3:30 a.m. They didn't want to miss seeing Terry.

Everyone was welcoming the entourage with open arms. Restaurant offered free meals.

Motels put us up, again free of charge. And the media was now showing up bigtime.

At 6 a.m. we were joined by a radio station news cruiser, then a second, and then a third. Local stations were assigning reporters to tag along with us for the whole day. Those radio station cruisers became our way of communicating to the public, in the age before social media, exactly where we were at on the road and when we'd be arriving in particular towns. Radio became indispensable to the Marathon of Hope.

At the breakfast break, the sides of the road were packed with well-wishers, all yelling encouragement—"You can do it, Terry," "We love you, Terry." Applause came from every direction, although there were always some people struck dumb, as I had been on my first day, just staring in wonder and awe at this kid with one leg give his all.

At the end of the day, we reached Oshawa and attended a reception at the Oshawa Centre Mall, welcomed by a drum and bugle corps, Mayor Jim Potticary, and 4,000 wildly cheering well-wishers. Terry was presented with a plaque on behalf of the city. We were gobsmacked by the sheer number of people. As usual, Terry expressed his appreciation in his speech and explained his mission. In all the interviews and speeches, it was some version of this: "My efforts may not result in finding a definitive cure, but only with research can we beat cancer. I'm not a dreamer, but I'm going to do whatever I can to find that cure."

The media attention kept growing as we got closer to Toronto. Sarah Purcell from the NBC prime-time television show *Real People* had arrived to tell Terry's story to the American public. Terry had been reluctant to participate when I first broached the idea. The show had massive ratings—fifteen to twenty-million viewers a week—but on occasion it made light of its subjects. He was concerned the meaning of his run might get lost. I told him I was confident that he'd be able to communicate his motives. He was handling the media attention well. Sarah ran with Terry and did an interview from a golf cart carrying a cameraman and sound person.

Terry enjoyed the experience. He smiled the whole time. Sarah asked real questions and he made her work by upping his running speed.

"This is a heck of a way to raise money," she said as she ran beside him.

"Things don't come easy," replied Terry.

The sound man running behind Sarah and Terry was the producer of the segment, a Canadian named John Brunton, who has since become one of Canada's most successful television producers. He remembers wiring Terry for sound to film the segment: "Late in the day, we were sitting quietly in the van. I saw Terry's stump dripping with blood.

I hadn't been prepared for the experience. I had never having met someone so humble, so pure, so self-effacing." Brunton was so impressed he would produce four more segments about Terry's run for *Real People*.

I'd had an idea in mind since New Brunswick that we could somehow get Rolly and Betty to fly out and surprise Terry in Toronto. With the help of the *Toronto Star*, I was able to set it up. On July 10, as the sun was rising, just before 6 a.m., Terry crested a small rise in the road and there, a block ahead, were his parents, standing in the middle of the road. Terry ran into his mother's arms and the three of them stood there hugging.

The image was on the *Star's* front page the next day. That illustrates how things were coming together for the Marathon of Hope. Earlier, we had been arranging everything that happened, coaxing people to share in the run. Now things were happening spontaneously and in every direction. The thing was taking on a life of its own.

Terry headed across the street for a quick visit with his parents at a Tim Horton's. He still had at another eighteen miles to complete on the day to stay on schedule. By the time he hit mile twelve and was ready for breakfast and his morning nap, he'd processed what had just happened. He and I were standing alone when he turned and said with some melancholy: "It's nice that they are here, but I won't have any time to spend with them."

That's how focused he was. Nothing was going to distract him, not even mom and dad. With that, he went for his nap and my mind started churning once again. When he got up, I took him aside and said: "I've got an idea. It's complicated but I think it will work. I'm going to change the entire schedule. We're going to stay an extra day in Toronto. We'll leave Sunday morning instead of Saturday afternoon."

I explained to him my plan for a visit to Niagara Falls. "I think we can fit it all in and still get your miles in," I said.

"If you can make it work, I'm in, but I still want to get my miles in," he smiled.

"Leave it with me," I said.

The Marathon of Hope was a roller coaster of extreme emotions, high and low. Seeing Terry with his parents was one of the highs. Later in the day came one of the lows.

We were at a rest stop near Pickering. A large crowd surrounded the van and Terry was open, at ease, chatting with everyone. I was at his side when a woman approached with a donation and quietly said to Terry: "You are running for my son."

Terry glanced around: "Where is he?"

"He passed away last month from cancer," she said, looking directly into Terry's eyes.

You never got used to that. As Terry comforted her, I turned and walked away. Choking back tears, I told one of the police officers, "I'll be back in a bit." I got in my car and cried for a long time.

I marvelled at how graciously Terry handled these moments. Most people don't realize that in addition to the physical pain of every step in his journey, he carried with him the hopes and tears of all the people he met along the way. It fuelled his purpose. He wasn't running for fame and fortune but for the kids back in the cancer ward and people like this bereft woman we met in Pickering. Running to give hope to them and all the other kids who would undoubtedly follow.

I drove a short distance away, went into a store, and bought a carton of popsicles. Back on the run, I passed them around to everyone on the crew, including the police officers.

I will never forget that day. It stoked my desire to support Terry and make his run a success. It still motivates me today to keep his legacy alive all these years later.

CHAPTER TEN

"Tell Me I'm Not Trying
Hard Enough"

IN RETROSPECT, THE CONCEPT OF it being Terry's run and only Terry's run perhaps was a little naïve.

As soon as you create something successful, everyone wants a piece of it. By the time we were approaching our weekend in the Greater Toronto Area, there wasn't enough Terry to go around.

It was a Thursday night when I called around to let everyone know I was altering the Toronto schedule to accommodate the Niagara excursion. Among other changes, we'd be dropping a Scarborough Civic Centre event on Friday. We simply couldn't fit it in. He had to show up early Friday to CTV's studio for an appearance on *Canada AM* and for a noon reception at Toronto City Hall, among other events. Most importantly, he still had to find time for Terry to run twenty-six miles, eat his meals, and take his naps. Nothing was going to get in the way of Terry's daily miles.

Everyone on the Thursday night call understood that Terry was stretched but the reaction to dropping the Scarborough event was dismay.

"You can't! You cannot just not show up. It would be a disaster," they pleaded.

In my head, I had a clear sense of which opportunities to prioritize. We couldn't pass up the *Canada AM* slot. It was the first chance for Terry to tell his story live to a national audience. The show had a massive following at the time. Terry's route had been designed to run through the center of Canada's media hub precisely for this reason. Toronto City Hall was obviously more important than the Scarborough Civic Centre, which might draw a couple thousand people. But the tone of the voices on the line was telling me that an accommodation had to be made.

I said, okay, we'd be there but we might be a little late.

"It doesn't matter, just be there, it's really important," I was told.

At that point, I was still fairly new to Toronto. I'd lived there for about six months and most of that time I'd been buried in work or on the road. I had little sense of the city's geography except for the routes to my downtown office and out to Welland. The GTA is a vast, sprawling entity that takes many years to appreciate.

While I was trying to keep these plates spinning on Thursday night, my friend Ray Bedard, who had been so useful with the Quebec police, was watching TV in my apartment. I'd asked him to be on hand for what I knew was going to be an incredibly hectic weekend. Without taking his eyes off the screen, he said calmly, "Do you realize that the CTV studio is across Highway 401 from the Civic Center? They're probably 10 minutes away from each other and you have a police escort."

That's why it's good to have a second brain working with you, someone to point out the obvious, especially when your own brain is overwhelmed by minutiae.

I immediately felt a rush of relief and the stress melting away: "We can do this," I thought. "We've got this!"

My next call was to Rick Guinan, whom I had worked with during my short stint as an insurance salesman on the Niagara Peninsula. I knew he had his pilot's license and I had spoken to him a month prior to broaching the idea of flying Terry over to Niagara Falls for a visit.

I told Rick it was on and asked if he could do it with short notice, say, Saturday afternoon?

His immediate response was "yes." He would have a plane ready at noon at the Toronto Island Airport. Boom, we had another box ticked on Terry's list.

Friday, July 11, turned out to be the second hottest day of the summer. The midday temperature would soar well about thirty degrees—a scorcher. Fortunately, the air at dawn was fresh and cool, perfect for a shortened morning run.

With the change in schedule, it was going to be a short day, eight miles with Terry finishing at Variety Village on Kingston Road. Variety Village is a world-class indoor sports facility built to nurture competitive spirits and empower children with disabilities—it was the perfect spot to end the run.

We were met at 5 a.m. by a police cruiser escort and two additional motorcycle police officers. I had a brief meeting with them and asked if they could keep Terry moving, stopping traffic at intersections. The answer was a friendly, "That's what we're here for."

Twenty-two-year-old Constable John Soffe, just a few months older than Terry, would remain with us for the entire day. He had been given the assignment by his sergeant the day before and had heard enough about the Marathon of Hope to be interested.

Terry finished his morning miles on time for the team to grab a quick breakfast at a restaurant in the Scarborough Town Centre. We'd pick up two more miles later in the day with the run to city hall, then return in

Saturday morning to complete the distance between Variety Village and the Four Seasons Hotel. With Const. Soffe and another motorcycle and police cruiser following, all with lights flashing, we were off to the CTV studios and Canada AM interview. The host was well prepared focusing in on why Terry was doing the run, asking him about the prosthesis, and how he faced his daily challenges.

Terry, as usual, was humble, sincere, and authentic. He spoke about his personal experience of cancer and what he'd seen in the children's ward. He was clear and articulate and every word came from the heart. It couldn't have gone better.

From the studio, it was off to the almost-cancelled Scarborough Civic Center reception. Now part of Toronto, Scarborough, at the time, was an independent municipality with its administration. As we drove up a circular driveway to its city hall, the streets were a mass of people. We now had three motorcycle officers, led by Constable Soffe. They were moving slowly ahead to open a pathway to the side entrance of the building. I kept thinking, "Wow, it would have been a major mistake on my part if we had actually pulled the plug."

Climbing out of the van, the mass of humanity made it near impossible to get to the doors of City Hall. Two very tall officers tried to gently push people back for Terry to make his way in. People were trying to hand Terry money, flowers, memorabilia, and get autographs signed. At one point, with no alternative, the police officers had to push back with a little force—they were worried that Terry might trip. Terry immediately grabbed my arm and quietly said: "Let them know it's ok." I think they overheard him and started taking gifts from the well-wishers and in turn handed them to him.

Inside the building, we were ushered into a side room and officially greeted by Deputy Mayor Shirley Eidt and Mayor Gus Harris who placed the mayor's chain of office on Terry's shoulders. The city presented Terry with a cheque for $5,000, but the most moving moment came when he was introduced to fourteen-year-old Anne Marie Von Zuben, who was wearing her Pathfinders uniform. She had been battling kidney cancer since the age of three and looked much younger than her age. When Terry leaned down to talk to her, she kissed him on the cheek and gave him a single daffodil. Terry was deeply affected by this simple gesture.

We walked a short distance into the main atrium of the Scarborough Civic Centre, which was packed with thousands of people. Although a large space, it had a warm feel to it. The several tiers of open balconies that surround the hall were crammed with people. Everyone was up close, with a good vantage point to see Terry. On the main floor, seated on the carpet, were at least 1,000 kids, part of the city's summer camp and recreation programs. A large banner hung from the wall—"Scarborough Welcomes Terry Fox"—but I remember better a sign held by a young boy: "Every Mile Wins a Smile." It was by far the largest indoor crowd that would greet him on his journey.

When he walked in, Terry received a thunderous round of applause that felt like it would never end. He could feel the love of the crowd. I saw it reflected in his warm smile. The only time he seemed a little uncomfortable was when the crowd began chanting his name.

In all the weeks I was with him, I never heard him speak with so much emotion as he did that day. He was on the verge of tears throughout the event. He relayed his usual message about cancer research but he also said some things that were new. He addressed his discomfort about the cult of personality that was growing up around him. Looking back, I think he was beginning to feel that people were losing sight of what his run was about. They were looking at him as a special person, a hero, and in his mind that was the worst thing that could become of his run.

He didn't want to be a symbol. He wanted to raise awareness and money for cancer research.

"For me," he said, "being famous is not the idea of the run and it wasn't from the very beginning. To me, the only important part of the publicity is that Cancer Can Be Beaten and the Marathon of Hope. I'm just one member of the Marathon of Hope. I'm no different than anyone else. I'm no better, I'm the same. I'm equal with all of you and if I ever change that attitude about myself there's no use in continuing."

He was being brutally honest and it sounded as though he was saying things that had been on his mind for some time.

His voice breaking, he continued: "So, when you are cheering and clapping for me, you are cheering and clapping for so many others who are involved in the run that no one hears about. The Cancer Society, the police and the volunteers. There's my brother Darrell, my friend, Doug, and Bill Vigars, who is the man from the cancer society. I'm trying my very best. I run all day and do publicity. Sometimes I have to change my schedule and [Bill] has to tell the people ahead of time and he gets all the shit and I don't think that's ok. If anyone complains about a change in schedule come up to me and tell me I'm not trying hard enough."

The last line was met with a short, stunned silence, then yells of "no," then more thunderous applause. I'm not sure how I felt what he said. I didn't like to be singled out and balancing the schedule was my job. I was getting paid for my trouble. At the same time, Terry grew up playing team sports. He was the ultimate team player and he was going to stick up for members of his team. I was not the only member of the team he would stand up for and we all appreciated that about him.

His speech ended on an ominous note. I didn't pick it up at the time. It was only years later when I watched a video of the occasion that

I heard it: "If for some reason I can't complete the run, it has to continue," he said. "Even if I don't finish it has to continue without me."

Those words sounded gallant to me in the moment. Through the lens of history, they are prophetic. They make me wonder if Big Jack was right and Terry knew or suspected something he wasn't sharing with us.

We made our way back to the van and headed off under police escort to the Four Seasons. I couldn't help but wonder at how things had changed. A few weeks back, we were in danger of getting kicked off the Quebec highways by law enforcement. Now we were heading down the Don Valley Parkway with a police cruiser and a motorcycle escort led by Constable Soffe. We weren't in Kansas anymore. He'd have to go back to Variety Village on the Saturday to pick up his run from where he left off.

Terry's fourteen-year-old sister, Judith, and his older brother, Fred, had also arrived the night before, along with Mom and Dad. Terry had about an hour to relax with his family in their suite. Our scheduled departure was 11:30 a.m.

Ray and I were sharing a room down the hall. While I was making calls, Roy was busy watching the Saturday morning cartoons, Rocky and Bullwinkle, one of my personal favourites, as well. There was a knock on the door. It was Darryl Sittler, standing there as large as life with a gym bag in one hand and a brown paper bag in another. The paper bag, I later found out, contained his 1980 NHL All-Star team sweater.

For those who don't follow the sport, Darryl Sittler is a Toronto hockey god. He played for the Toronto Maple Leafs from 1970 to 1985 and was elected to the Hockey Hall of Fame in 1989, the Ontario Sports Hall of Fame in 2003, and Canada's Walk of Fame in 2016. He has since made the list of one of the 100 Greatest NHL Players in history. At the time we met him in Toronto, Sittler still held the NHL record for most points by a player in a single game—the famous ten-point game.

And here he was. Hockey royalty, knocking at my hotel room door. He had to change into some running gear so I beckoned him in and turned to Ray and said, "We have to get out for a moment, Darryl has to change."

Ray protested: "But it's my room."

"Come on, Ray," I insisted. "Let's go.

Ray was maybe the one person in Ontario who had never heard of Darryl Sittler. He was no sports fan. He was into boating.

So, as Sittler steps into the room, Ray reluctantly gets up and politely shakes Darryl's hand, introducing himself and asking our guest his name.

"Ah, Darryl Sittler."

"And what do you do?"

"I play hockey."

"Oh, who for?"

"Toronto Maple Leafs."

"Ah, my dad watches them."

And with that, Ray turns and leaves. To this day, I cringe about their conversation.

When we were outside of the room, I looked at Ray, incredulous.

"WHAT?!?" I asked.

"Sorry, I don't watch hockey," said Ray, nonchalantly. "Now if he wants to go fishing..."

Moments later, Darryl came out of the room wearing shorts, running shoes, and a t-shirt. I took him down the hall and as we entered the room, he greeted Terry: "Ok, who wants to go for a run?"

Another wish comes true for Terry.

There were a lot of people in the suite, including Izzy Sharp, our benefactor and owner of the Four Seasons hotel chain, and his public relations expert, the invaluable Bev Norris. Bev was not only managing VIP receptions but taking good care of the whole Fox family.

After a few moments, I announced that it was time to roll and we all headed towards the elevators. We went down to the lobby with Sittler, actor Al Waxman, star of *The King of Kensington*, and Paul Godfrey, who was then the Metro Toronto chairman.

Outside, a phalanx of police was at the ready, along with a promotional van belonging to a beer company. The van had a speaker system that was blaring a song called "Run Terry Run," by the Nancy Ryan Singers. In a very short period of time, it seemed every radio station in Ontario was playing the song and we'd hear it at almost every event we attended, so you can imagine we were all soon sick of it, even while appreciating the great tribute it paid to Terry and the Marathon of Hope.

Also part of the procession were a number of young volunteers, including Jeremy Brown's two sons, fifteen-year-old Karl and twelve-year-old Jonathan. Someone had handed the volunteers green garbage bags with which to collect donations.

"Let's roll!" I shouted to Constable Soffe.

He pulled out of the hotel's driveway and immediately found a truck partially blocking our way. In a thundering voice, he yelled to the driver, "Move your ass!" Obediently the driver put his truck in reverse and backed into a taxi cab.

Oops.

"I'll call it in," Soffe yelled, and kept us moving. A lone female officer stood in the Intersection, stopping traffic on Avenue Road stood with her mouth agape at what had just happened.

Our route would take us south on Avenue Road towards City Hall, crossing Bloor Street and on through Queen's Park Circle, which wraps around the Provincial Legislature. On the other side of the circle, Avenue Road becomes University Avenue, a grand eight-line boulevard with a broad median containing memorials, status, gardens, and fountains. On either side are some of Canada's leading research hospitals, including what is now called the Princess Margaret Cancer Centre, one of the world's leading cancer research facilities and one that benefits to this day from the Marathon of Hope.

With the flashing lights of the police vehicles leading the way, Terry ran alone, followed closely by Darrell, Darryl Sittler, and Doug—a hockey fan who had left the driving on this day to Ray. As we came out of the circle on to University Avenue, the scene was unreal. I still get shivers thinking about it. The road was lined with thousands of people. It seemed as though every window of the large buildings to either side was full of waving, cheering people. A young girl on roller-skates kept pace with Terry, a respectful distance to his right.

I was running along, moving from the front to the side to the rear and then back to catch up with Terry. I was sweating buckets, as we all were. At one point, with the beer van still blaring "Run Terry Run," Terry smiled and yelled at me: "If I hear that song one more time, I'm going to shoot somebody."

Darrell and Sittler ran side by side. Women were yelling "Darryl! Darryl!" With his usual humour, Darrell teased the older hockey star that the younger women were actually yelling "Darrell!" If it was an older woman, he would say "That one's for you."

Const. Soffe, astride motorcycle 9401, led the procession through a left turn at the corner of Queen Street to head a block east to Nathan Philips Square. The bikes pulled onto the sidewalk at the west end of the City Hall Plaza. It was a heaving sea of people—pure bedlam with music playing, people yelling and clapping. Doug, who by this time had jumped back behind the wheel of the van, was frantically calling to me: "What do I do with the van, where do I park?"

I motioned to him to pull up on to the sidewalk.

"I can't park there," he said.

"Yes, you can. We park anywhere. We're with Terry," I shouted.

Still Doug hesitated until one of the policemen pointed to the same spot I was motioning towards.

Terry was still running so the policemen jumped off their bikes to clear a path for him through the crowd. People were reaching out to touch him, some trying to give him money, religious items, flowers, flags—everything imaginable, as if he were some kind of saint or deity. Terry would cringe at the analogy but people reacted that way.

I managed to get myself between Terry and the police, moving backwards so that Terry could pass the items thrust into his hands to me. I then handed them off to Canadian Cancer Society volunteers who seemed to appear out of nowhere. Out of nowhere, a female photographer stepped in between me and Terry. I could tell from the equipment slung over her shoulders that she was a professional on assignment and that she was getting some amazing shots. By luck I noticed a large black cable, obviously from one of the television stations broadcasting live, stretched in our path. I somehow stepped over it when I saw the photographer's heel strike the cable and she started to fall backward. I reached down and caught her before she hit the concrete and was able to throw her back up to a standing.

"Keep going," I yelled at her. The noise from the crowd was deafening.

She did. Thus started my lifelong friendship with the great news photographer Gail Harvey.

As Terry ascended the stairs to the stage, 10,000 souls let lose the biggest cheer I've ever experienced in person. The skyscrapers surrounding us seemed to amplify the sound. I was standing off to the side with Ray, looking at Terry surrounded by his whole family and an array of dignitaries. Al Waxman was at the microphone and still had to yell to be heard over the crowd: "Ladies and gentleman, Terry Fox!" The crowd went wild. I imagine that's what it will sound like some day if the Leafs ever win the Stanley Cup.

I was especially grateful to see Jeremy Brown up there on stage. "You did it, sir," I said to myself. "You and your team came through. I'll never be able to thank you enough."

I was exhausted, completely spent from just that hour on the sweltering pavement, but happy on so many levels. After Canada AM, Scarborough, and this reception at Toronto City Hall, I was confident that all of Canada would soon know about the Marathon of Hope. They would be believers in this kid from Port Coquitlam and his mission to make a difference in the fight against cancer, which is all he wanted.

It was perfect. But there were many more miles on the road ahead.

CHAPTER ELEVEN

Heroes and Bumper Cars

BEFORE HE WENT TO BED at the end of that wild July 11, I was able to tell Terry that the Canadian Cancer Society had raised an estimated $100,000 in Toronto. I had to say it twice and assure him that I wasn't kidding. Of that amount, $59,000 came from CKFM, Jeremy Brown's radio station (it would eventually raise $500,000 for the Marathon of Hope).

I was incredibly proud of him on the day. He spoke well and handled himself graciously, even if he was getting more personal attention than he wanted or thought he deserved. I can't stress enough that he didn't want the glory. He was running for a cause.

Darryl Sittler had been a little late to the Four Seasons that morning because he went back home to get a gift for Terry. He wasn't sure what to bring but ultimately decided on his all-star jersey. He presented it to Terry on stage. Terry immediately put it on. At one point, Rolly took Terry's hand and lifted his arm high in the air like a champion. There were great cheers. Terry quickly brought his arm back down, uncomfortable with being hailed as a hero.

"What struck me most about Terry," said Sittler, "was what a humble individual he was. No ego, and completely focused on his goal."

As things were winding down on stage, the photographer I had caught in the melee of our arrival tapped me on the shoulder, introduced herself as Gail Harvey of United Press Canada and said: "I'm wondering if it would be possible for me to join Terry on the road for a couple of days to takes some pictures of his Marathon of Hope?"

She had a pleasant demeanour and I liked that she had used the term "Marathon of Hope" right off the bat. I told her I would have to speak to Terry. We were heading inside city hall for a press conference and if she would wait around until we were finished, I'd let her know. "I'll see you at the press conference," she said.

Constable Soffe had taken the reins and led Terry, Al Waxman, Darryl Sittler, and Metro Council Chairman Paul Godfrey towards the front doors of city hall. With the crowds once again surging to try to shake Terry's hand or present him with something, it was again slow going but the five eventually rode the elevator to the executive office area.

The reception from the press that day was unlike anything I ever encountered. I had been an elected official at age twenty-two and a news reporter before that, working for a local radio station and as a stringer in Southwestern Ontario for the *Globe & Mail*. I'd seen the media in action and I knew reporters could be a cynical lot. Yet that day they appeared in awe of Terry, much like the general public.

The questions were respectful and there were no attempts to embarrass him or the Marathon of Hope. Terry was given plenty of time to speak and tell his story. He said that he was often tired on the run and that he knew he could quit anytime he wanted to, but the kids back in the BC cancer ward couldn't quit and that's what drove him.

The reporters did try to get Terry to talk about himself and explain his inner thoughts. I've seen experienced politicians stumble off message under the glare of television lights and with the distraction of microphones thrust in their faces. Terry had never had any media training but he communicated like a pro—a complete natural. He would only say that he had been an athlete all his life and that running was something he could do to make a difference—there was nothing more to his story. He steered the conversation back to cancer and fundraising. And he did it with such heart-warming sincerity that it melted any hint of cynicism in the room.

As that event started wrapping up, Constable Soffe, who had been our guardian angel for the past thirteen hours came to ask what was next on the agenda. I told him our official day was done and we were all headed back to the Four Seasons. He shook my hand and said he was off, taking time to say good bye to Terry before departing. I never had a chance to thank him myself until more than forty years later when I tracked him down in Peterborough while researching this book. Thank you, again, Constable John Soffe. You wore your badge well.

I had a quick moment to talk to Terry after the press conference about the possibility of a news photographer joining us on the road to document his journey. He agreed but wanted to wait until we were out of Toronto. I pointed out Gail to him. She introduced herself and arrangements were made for me to contact her when we got past Barrie in a couple of weeks.

Back at the hotel, Terry had time to shower and rest and spend time with his family. That night, he would throw out the opening pitch at the Toronto Blue Jays game to a standing ovation.

With Terry's approval, Ray and I headed off in the now-iconic Marathon Hope van for the ninety-minute drive to Welland on the Niagara Peninsula. We wanted to show off the vehicle to Ray's little brother,

Marc, and Ray's parents. Marc had been following Terry's journey from afar and couldn't believe it when we pulled up in the family's driveway. It was a whirlwind trip with a half-hour stopover and I think we were back at the hotel in Toronto by 9 p.m. that evening.

Terry's schedule for Saturday allowed him a rare break from the 4 a.m. alarm. We had carved out time for a quick visit to Niagara Falls. My friend, Rick Guinan, along with his friend and the photographer for the trip, Floyd Brooks, met us at the Toronto Island Airport in a Piper Cherokee Archer four-seat airplane for the 10:30 a.m. departure. Rick's first glimpse of Terry was of a young man walking towards the plane, surrounded by people clapping, shaking his hand, and pushing donations at him. Rick's reaction echoed Darryl Sittler's: "It was quite amazing and I was impressed of how humble and down to earth he was. He had a big smile that I'll never forget."

Terry hopped into the passenger seat and Rick explained the controls to Terry's great interest. Taking off on Runway 30, they circled over the water front, then banked and headed west towards Hamilton, hugging the shoreline since the flight plan wouldn't allow crossing the water.

As they passed through Hamilton airspace, a voice from the control tower welcomed the flight with a short phrase: "I understand you have precious cargo on board."

It was a whirlwind tour and, in some aspects, slightly disappointing. The local Optimist Club had financed the flight and a good number of members met Terry on arrival. The Optimists are just as they sound, a worldwide volunteer organization of more than 2,500 local clubs whose goal is to make the future brighter by bringing out the best in their members, their communities, and in youth. They're glass-half-full people and they take their cause seriously.

Unfortunately, on that particular day, very few people had been made aware of Terry's plans.

The district director of the Canadian Cancer Society, who was about to became a major pebble in our shoe, had not notified local volunteers. Nonetheless, several individuals from the Optimists Club stepped up and were so impressed by Terry that they made him a lifetime member.

His first visit was to a small reception at the historic Prince of Wales Hotel in Niagara-On-The-Lake. From there, we went to Niagara Falls to visit city hall. It hadn't helped that the local director had failed to organize things on the ground, but ultimately it was my screw-up. I hadn't done the most basic advance work that a public relations manager should have done to lay the ground work for Terry's visit. With so much going on, it just got by me. Thankfully, no one noticed. Well, not Wayne Thomson, Niagara's mayor at the time, although he had only been told of the visit the day before. He still vividly remembers greeting Terry at city hall. "He was very bright and very articulate," recalls Thomson, who in five decades as a public official had met countless prime ministers and celebrities, but never someone like Terry.

"For me personally," says Thomson, "it was probably the most important event that I had during my public life. He was very impressive, and what has happened in the ensuring years, and what he accomplished regarding research into cancer, and the money that has been raised across Canada is second to none."

Despite the poor planning, there were two shining moments during the visit. First, Terry was able to hook up with Jay Triano, his pal from Simon Fraser University. Jay was a big reason that Terry wanted to go to Niagara Falls, where the Trianos are a sports dynasty (Jay's brother Jeff was drafted by the Toronto Maple Leafs). "We had a casual talk about his run," Jay remembered in a TSN interview. "He talked over and over about the prosthetic leg and the grinding and chasing that was going on there and how painful it was but he was just bound and determined he was never going to stop his run."

Terry also spent time that day with nineteen-year-old Steve Iorio, who also had lost his leg to osteosarcoma. They discussed their common experiences and Iorio later credited the time they spent together with giving him the strength and courage to overcome his health obstacles.

The day did not end well. When Steve, Terry, and the Canadian Cancer Society volunteers headed to Marineland, a local tourist attraction featuring performing orcas, seals, and dolphins, he was asked to pose for a promotional picture. Terry immediately cut the visit short. He was pissed at being used for commercial purposes. Again, my fault for not checking everything out beforehand. Rick was called and Terry returned to the airport to head back to the city; he still had to finish his miles that afternoon.

By 2.30 p.m., that afternoon, he was back at the hotel. I was waiting for him in the lobby, and he made a beeline for me. "You didn't tell me it was a small plane," he said. "Not only that, when we got to Niagara Falls the pilot decided to give me a good view and did two tight circles right over the falls. It scared the shit out of me!"

He was only half-joking. He later explained how frightened he'd been to be staring straight down at the falls as the plane did a tight bank. I shared this with Rick, who laughed: "Sorry I couldn't get a 747—it was the best I could do!" He also explained that he wasn't goofing around with Terry in the plane: there was a specific flight route to be followed over the falls and he followed it.

Saturday afternoon, it was back to business. Terry had to cover the distance we had skipped the day before from Variety Village to the Four Seasons Hotel. It was a short six miles but Terry had to adjust his headspace from glad-handing to the grind of the road. It was hot and humid and the city's pavement reflected the heat back up at him.

The route took us down the Danforth, a major east-west avenue dating back to 1799 and named for the engineer Asa Danforth who also built portions of Toronto's Queen Street East and Kingston Road using wood planks. The Danforth starts at Broadview Ave on the top flank of the Don River's eastern bank and runs east in a straight line to Scarborough. At that time, and still to some extent now, the Danforth had a small town feel to it, with numerous restaurants and bars and small family-run stores, apartments above. Most of the restaurants were Greek, thus the name for the section from Broadview to Pape Avenue is Greektown.

Word of mouth and radio reports attracted a big crowd and the Danforth was lined three and four people deep along the entire stretch, right up to where it crosses over the Don Valley and becomes Bloor Street East. It seemed as though every patron of every restaurant and drinking establishment put down their beers and came out to see the kid. The money poured it, later at the hotel we counted over $5,000, not including the cash we were continually handing over to Canadian Cancer Society volunteers.

Terry ran up Bloor Street to its intersection with Yonge Street and then on to the Four Seasons. We all headed to our rooms to freshen up except Ray Bedard, who was sitting in the lobby when two police officers came in with Doug, who had been running along the route like the rest of us collecting donations. He'd been trailing some distance behind us and missed the turn to the hotel that we had made. Three blocks down the street a police cruiser pulled over and asked him what he was doing. The officers thought he might be collecting money to line his own pockets. He was loaded into the back of the cruiser and taken red-faced to the hotel lobby. It was a great opportunity to play a prank—"never seen him before, officers"—but Ray rightly played it straight and Terry's good friend and right-hand man headed up to his room.

Terry spent some more time with his family that evening, dining atop the CN Tower—another item ticked off his original list. The tower was lit up with the words, "Welcome Terry Fox."

That was special to me, indicating that we'd arrived and made a mark that could be seen all across Canada's largest city.

While the rest of the entourage were eating, an exhausted Terry fell asleep on his mother's shoulder. I remember being touched at the sight of mother and son sharing a quiet moment. It struck me how worried Betty must have been watching her son push himself so hard, day after day.

There was one last bit a fun to wrap up the evening. After his brief nap, Terry and the gang headed down to the small amusement park in the bowels of the CN Tower. The main attraction was the bumper cars. Terry and the others skidded around on a metal floor in electrified, padded cars, smashing into each other, having a great time. It was great to see Terry, a grown man of twenty-two, having already fought a life-and-death battle with cancer, behaving like a kid. He may have been wise beyond his years, but when his face lit up in that boyish grin, he looked like a kid and that's probably why he'll probably always be a kid in our memories.

At one point, Darrell managed to broadside Terry's car so hard that his artificial leg popped off. He had a hell of time disentangling it from his pants leg. When he finally got it out, he climbed out of the car and using the prothesis as a cane, hopped across the floor, whereupon everyone in the place suddenly recognized him. "It's Terry Fox!" And he was mobbed all over again.

CHAPTER TWELVE

"For God's Sake, Stop!"

A FTER TWO HECTIC DAYS IN Toronto, we woke up on Sunday morning to find the city's streets quiet and mostly empty. I didn't mind. I felt nothing buy joy and satisfaction about how things were going for Terry and the Marathon of Hope.

At 9:30 a.m., Terry and the crew returned to a deserted Nathan Phillips Square where he had ended his run the day before. A contingent of Toronto's finest was ready to protect and serve Terry. He was eager to get back into his regular running routine.

We headed south the few blocks to Lakeshore Boulevard from City Hall, turning right on a route that would lead us to Oakville and Hamilton and up Highway 2 to London.

Lake Shore runs west parallel to Lake Ontario on its south side and the massive Gardiner Expressway to the north. As Terry ran down Lake Shore, brothers Fred and Darrell, myself, and a few others running behind to collect donations, the lead motorcycle officer pointed Terry towards the entrance ramp to the Gardiner.

"Where the hell are we going?" I wondered.

I was right behind Terry as we reach the top of the ramp. I could see they had closed the entire expressway—multiple lanes in both directions. I was stunned. And there were no angry, honking drivers at the closed entry ramps. Rather, people were emptying out of their vehicles either to stand and clap or to line the route and cheer.

A heavily travelled highway, the Gardiner is a magnet for outdoor advertising—gigantic electronic signs flash messages to millions of passing motorists in either direction. In the early stages of organizing Terry's journey through Ontario, I had come up with the idea of approaching the companies that owned those signs to display some type of welcoming message for Terry while he was in Toronto. As mentioned before, I'm a pretty good ideas man but execution is not my strong suit. I'd pretty much forgotten the idea. Fortunately, the dependable Deborah Kirk had not. She spoke to every one of those companies a month earlier and now all those signs were flashing a variation of "Welcome Terry" as we came up to the roadway.

I've often wondered how Terry must have felt coming up that ramp to those giant signs flashing his name and message as people cheered from lines that stretched as far as the eye can see. On other occasions, he acknowledged that the reception he received from folks along the route, the shouts of encouragement and financial support, boosted his mindset while running. "It takes away the pain often," he said, "Sometimes I just find myself floating with that support." I'm sure he felt both gratitude and validation as he ran along the Gardiner. The sight of him running under those great flashing signs will stay with me forever.

By early afternoon, we had crossed through Etobicoke, the municipality to the west of Toronto, and reached the eastern edge of Mississauga where the Peel Regional Police would take over escort duties from Toronto's constabulary. Terry took his lunch break then headed for his mid-day nap. I said goodbye to Ray.

After serving the Marathon of Hope to great effect in Quebec and Toronto, Ray was going back to his own life. We sat at a picnic table near a creek in a small park adjacent to Terry's hotel and reminisced about our adventures. He said the experience had left him a life-time's worth of memories. And he was right. Ray and I drifted apart over the years but when I called him to check some details and supplement my own memories of our time together for this book, he was a font of information and his recollection of events was often sharper than mine. I also learned that a photo of Ray protecting Terry from an annoying photographer during the run still hangs in his living room. Like all of us, he is amazed at his good fortune in being a small part of the history Terry was making.

I could see that while he was glad to re-establish his routine on the road, it wasn't easy for Terry. Just as in Montreal, the break from his daily mileage and the additional rest had thrown him off stride. He was struggling towards the end of the day and a scheduling mishap didn't help matters.

We were near the end of the day's run with one event on our schedule. At a park in Mississauga, we were greeted by the mayor, "Hurricane Hazel" McCallion, who been elected two years earlier and would remain in office for a staggering thirty-six years until her retirement in 2014.

"Canada needed something, and you've done it," she said to Terry.

With the ceremonies concluded, we were about to go back on the highway to do three more miles so Terry could complete his full twenty-six when we learned that the meeting with Hazel hadn't been the one on our schedule. It seems a district director of the Canadian Cancer Society had arranged the Hazel event without telling us. The real reception was down the highway at Sheridan College in Oakville. It had been organized by Canadian Cancer Society volunteer Joan Gibb, who had been a major supporter of the Marathon of Hope at that crucial April meeting in the Westbury Hotel.

I was furious about the double booking and made my views known to people in the Canadian Cancer Society. It seemed so disrespectful of a guy who was running—this can't be repeated often enough—*a marathon a day* not for his own glory but for the cause of cancer research. The discussion got heated and I was threatened with being reported to headquarters. We had little choice but to go through with the second event. Terry soldiered on. He made a wonderful speech at Sheridan College and then went back to where he'd stopped running to finish those three miles.

The whole thing added an extra forty-five minutes to his already long day which, again, was hot and humid. We finally got Terry into the van and headed to the Holiday Inn in Oakville. He was in a bad mood as we were unloading in the parking lot and told me in no uncertain terms: "It's one reception. Only one. That's the rule, that's the agreement!"

I didn't argue with him. My job in the moment was to receive his anger. Maybe I should have been more on the ball, or pushed back harder, but I think I was intimidated by the threat of being reported to headquarters. I had already heard rumours that some of the other department heads at Ontario Division were complaining about the amount of time I was spending away from the office. I was getting paid by the Canadian Cancer Society, but Terry had my complete attention.

By the time he showered and we were at dinner, the matter was dead and talked only of the good parts of the day. Terry's temper was like that: he only expressed it when he had a legitimate reason and, as quickly as it surfaced, it was gone. We learned to take it in the spirit of teamwork: our captain was pushing us to up our game. I still walked with him to his room after dinner and apologized again for the screw up.

In addition to Terry readjusting to his road routine, we were all adjusting to a new reality in the Marathon of Hope. Way back in New Brunswick when Terry and I first laid out the schedule, I had two key dates: July 1 in Ottawa and July 11 in Toronto. We had high hopes for those dates but no way of knowing if we'd have any success or how the public would be viewing Terry and his run if and when we made them. So we had no set schedule beyond Toronto. No next milestone to look forward to and gear up for. It meant no pressure and that bothered us all.

It especially bothered Terry. He thrived on pressure. He was a goal-oriented athlete who craved the pressure that comes from competition—even if he was only competing with himself. Terry could not get it out of his mind that there was now nothing ahead on the schedule, no pressure to make a big event. It weighed heavily on him for the rest of the run and my efforts to dispel that notion were never entirely successful.

He craved the challenge but he was a pro and when the time came to step out on the road, he was always ready, no complaints, no second thoughts. It was always, game on.

All he could see ahead of him was a lot of running. A big loop to London in Southern Ontario to London before heading up to Sudbury and across the emptiness of Northern Ontario through Sault Ste. Marie to Thunder Bay, then the prairie provinces, then the Rockies and British Columbia. We were already in mid-July. There was no specific date by which the run was supposed to end—back on Highway 7, Terry had mused in an interview about reaching BC in mid-November—but by spending so much time in Southern Ontario, it was looking like he might be running through Alberta in the snow.

Running as far west as London added an onerous load on to the schedule, but Terry realized that close to 40 percent of Canada's population lived in Southern Ontario and he wanted to maximize the fundraising opportunity. Before we had even reached Toronto, I had suggested to Terry that once he'd run to London he should drive back to Toronto and run north from there. Backtracking east from London seemed like a waste of time and energy. But Terry wouldn't hear of it. The route was the route: he had laid it down with Ron Calhoun months earlier. Betty and Rolly Fox hadn't raised a shirker and you didn't argue with Terry once his mind was made up. "I don't want anyone to be able to say that I did not cover every step of the way," he insisted.

We pushed ahead to Oakville. This stretch of the run, perhaps more than any other, impressed upon me that the Marathon of Hope was also about the people we met along the way. One of these was Peter Martyn, a twenty-three-year-old photographer for the *Oakville Journal Record*. Early that morning, July 14, he took a picture that would change his life. He stood in the middle of the glistening wet road with Terry running towards him and captured Terry's unmistakable figure silhouetted in the dark by the headlights of the police cruiser behind him. Peter went back to the office and showed the image to his editor, who chose not to use it—"You can't see his face." Undeterred, Peter sent the photo to the Canadian Press wire service. The editors there loved it. It went out on the wire and, as he recalls, "suddenly it had legs and began appearing everywhere." It was chosen as the Canadian Press photo of the year. Peter moved up to the *Edmonton Journal* and, subsequently, the *Montreal Gazette*, and now has galleries in Canada, Britain, and the US.

Towards the end of the day as we approached Burlington, there were so many people along the road that we couldn't collect all the donations. We shouted into the crowd: "We need ten volunteers!"

Among the many who stepped forward were two who seemed especially excited to join the crew. They were literally jumping up and down. One was Cam Morrison, who would later join us for a few days in Muskoka. The other was Glemena Bettencourt, who had been collecting funds for Terry in a goldfish bowl after reading about the Marathon of Hope in the newspapers. She was a quintessential "Foxer," which is what we called our super-volunteers. She would often drive out to wherever we were to join the run for a day and she would later be instrumental in getting a memorial statue of Terry installed at Richmond Hill.

At Burlington, we were informed that there would be a reception for Terry at the Royal Botanical Gardens. This was a surprise to me, but a nice one—we had nothing else on the agenda—and satisfying given that Burlington was part of the Hamilton divisions of the Canadian Cancer Society that a few months earlier had wanted nothing to do with the Marathon of Hope.

Standing at the side of the road as we approached the gardens was Ron Foxcroft, a cornerstone of both the Hamilton and Burlington communities, having been named citizen of the year by both. In addition to being president of a large trucking company and the inventor of the Fox 40 whistle that is used in many major sporting events, Ron was a referee in the NBA and at the Olympics (he was assigned the infamous gold medal basketball came between the US and Russia in 1976—the only official both sides could agree on). He remembers Terry's appearance as though it were yesterday:

Everyone knew he was coming. It was everywhere in the news, radio stations were broadcasting where he was. My office was on Plains Road and I remember standing out there waiting for him. It was a beautiful sunny day, the street was lined with crowds. It was like the Christmas Parade in July.

He struck me as an inspiration in so many good ways, a selfless individual going to the limit for healthcare and cancer research.

Terry Fox, age twenty-one (photo by Michael Flomen).

With longtime friend Doug Alward after dipping his leg in the Atlantic Ocean at St. John's, Newfoundland, April 12, 1980.

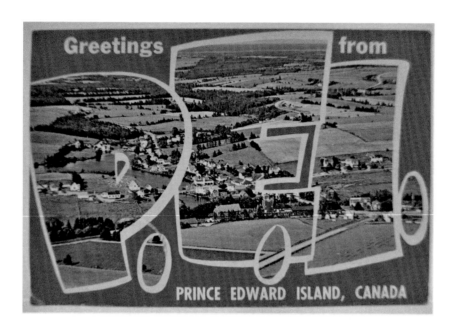

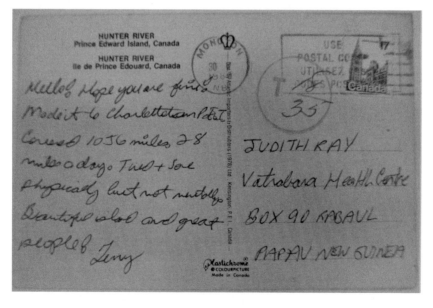

One of a series of postcards to Judith Ray, Terry's nurse at Royal Columbian hospital. She was among his earliest and biggest supporters. Terry was enjoying seeing Canada throughout the Marathon of Hope.

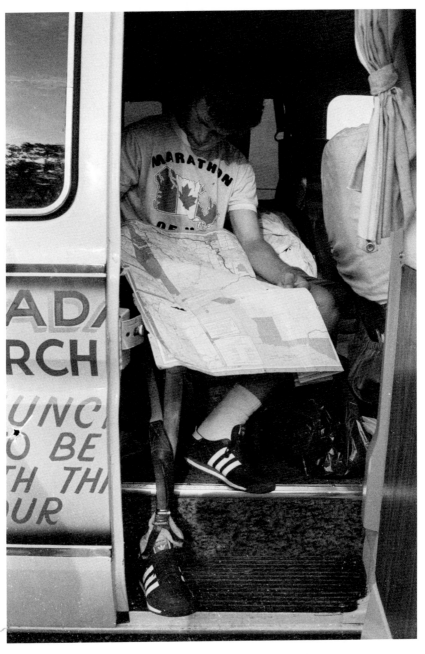

In the days before smartphones and GPS, Terry and his crew navigated with big folding roadmaps (photo by Gail Harvey.)

A frame-by-frame demonstration of Terry's running gait captured by filmmaker John Simpson.

Terry's artificial leg was crude by modern standards but advanced for its time. It was designed with a spring to ensure it snapped back in place after each forward step and a waist strap to hold it in place (photo by Gail Harvey).

(Top) Running in the summer heat, Terry took regular hydration breaks, often aided by his brother Darrell (photo by Gail Harvey). (Below) Bill Vigars had to keep up with Terry on the road and finished the summer in the best shape of his life (photo by Gail Harvey).

(Top) There were grave concerns for Terry's safety as he ran along the sides of highways frequented by large transport trucks. (Below) In Ontario, a daily police escort protected both Terry and the people who came out to see him on his route (photo by Michael Flomen).

A marathon a day required fuel. Terry ate a lot at every meal (photo by Gail Harvey).

Canadian Cancer Society District directors Jack Lambert and Lou Fine share a joke with Patrick Vigars while Doug Awlard looks on. At the back, Kerry Anne Vigars watches Bill and Terry play catch the french fry. (French River Trading Post. Credit Gail Harvey).

Terry, along with brother Darrell, Doug Alward, and Patrick and Kerry Ann Vigars, met Prime Minister Pierre Trudeau in Ottawa (photo courtesy of Government of Canada Archives).

Nathan Phillips Square at Toronto City Hall was packed with Terry Fox fans on July 12. The massive media coverage lifted the Marathon of Hope to a new level (photo by Gail Harvey).

Terry ran down Toronto's University Avenue with hockey great Darryl Sittler at his side and Queen's Park in the background. Leading the procession is Toronto police officer John Soffe on his motorcycle (photo by Gail Harvey).

Peter Martin, a twenty-three-year-old photographer for the *Oakville Journal Record*, took this early morning shot of Terry. It was chosen as the Canadian Press photo of the year.

Terry tended to guard his privacy but quickly came to trust photographer Gail Harvey, who shot a series of pictures of him in his roadside hotel room at the end of a day's run.

There were moments of tension and sadness on the road but also much laughter, often inspired by Terry himself. (Top) Clowning with a raccoon hat at the French River trading post (photo by Gail Harvey). (Bottom) Posing with the toilet seat presented to him by his crew and other volunteers to mark his twenty-second birthday in Gravenhurst.

No single image captures Terry's concentration better than this now iconic shot by Gail Harvey. It has been published everywhere and until recently was featured in Canadian passports.

Long portions of Terry's run were completed on lonely stretches of highway and he often started before the sun was up. Gail Harvey captured this image one misty dawn.

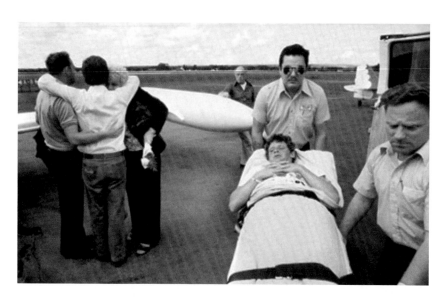

At the end of the Marathon of Hope, Terry was loaded onto a medivac flight in Thunder Bay. Bill Vigars embraces Rolly and Betty Fox while Lou Fine, a Canadian Cancer Society director, leans on the wing and looks on in dismay (photo by David Cooper, Gerry Images).

It was only a few minutes in my lifetime but it has stuck with me for the re-set of my life. I've thought if I could be just 10 percent of him, I could do some good with my own life. I've dealt with people from around the world in my business and they view Canadians as leader, honest, sensitive and reliable. Terry was all of those things. I think of him and that day often.

Cars lined the side of the road for at least a mile leading to the entrance of the Royal Botanical Gardens. The parking lot with buses and vehicles. The crowd was enormous and as Terry arrived, the Burlington Teen Tour Marching band, 150 members strong, greeted him with an energetic rendition of George Gershwin's "Strike up The Band."

The band included a number of baton-twirling majorettes, among them fifteen-year-old Kristy Smith. Her family lived in Oakville and earlier that morning she had run down to Lakeshore to see Terry run by. The sight of him sent chills down her spine. She was an athlete as a youth and is still active today. She realized the strength and fortitude required to run a marathon. That he was doing it with an artificial leg and was running in shorts that unabashedly showing that leg blew her away. "No one ever did that that I could remember." Six hours later, after the band had paraded out, she sat on the ground with other performers to hear Terry speak. "It was a privilege that I did not totally appreciate until years later. I'll never forget that day."

For Terry, the highlight of the reception was meeting Burlington native Gord Dickson, an inaugural member of the Canadian Road Running Hall of Fame. Over the years, Gord had won six Canadian Marathon Championships, a bronze medal in the 1959 Pan Am Games, and he had participated in the 1960 Olympics despite an Achilles heel injury.

As Terry neared the Burlington-Hamilton area, Gord knew he had to do something. At the last Minute, he grabbed his 1960 Canadian Marathon Gold Medal and had Terry's name inscribed on it before rushing to the Botanical Gardens reception. He presented it to Terry on stage. Terry deeply appreciated this gesture by one of his kind and treasured the medal as a recognition of his athletic ability.

We were soon off again and not far down the road Terry met someone who would touch him as deeply as anyone along the trail. Greg Scott was a ten-year-old all-star baseball player from Welland (his family, coincidentally, lived on the same street I'd lived on in Welland). Greg and Terry had the same type of cancer and had both lost a leg, Terry his right, Greg his left.

Greg and his family had waited three hours on Dundurn Street to that he could meet his hero. Theor connection was immediate and they would eventually develop a close friendship. They joked about losing their hair and Terry told Greg about having to wear a bad wig until his grew back, much curlier than before. The camaraderie between two cancer survivors was palpable. Everyone standing nearby could feel it. We couldn't help but be impressed by the sparkle in Greg's eyes, his admiration for Terry, and Terry's affection for him. It was a magical moment.

Of course, we soon had to move on—more miles to run—but Terry would ask me daily if I had any news on Greg. I was able to report that Greg's treatment was progressing and that I'd started to lay the groundwork for another meeting between the two of them down the road.

There was one other interaction on that day that stands out to me as vividly as anything else I experienced with Terry. It happened in Burlington and it began with yelling.

"Stop, stop! For God's sake, stop! They're using you! They're using you!"

I was running behind Terry, collecting donations, and I could hear the voice—it belonged to a woman—but I couldn't see her. She sounded both angry and pleading at the same time. I searched the busy intersection as Terry was making a left hand turn off of Plains Road and spotted her: a middle-aged woman who had stopped her car in the middle of the road. She had rolled down her window and was yelling as loud as she could at Terry. In fact, she was screaming at him. Most troubling were her words: "They're using you, they're using you!"

In a split second, I realized she was distressed, thinking that Terry was injuring himself running a marathon a day. She was under the impression the Canadian Cancer Society or some other force was making him push himself to the limit.

It was all happening fast and in the midst of heavy traffic. Even with the police escort, it felt dangerous. My immediate thought was for Terry. I should have known that he would take it in stride, literally.

Terry never stopped running. It was another hard and fast rule. He only stopped at his mile or two-mile rest breaks. Terry did not break stride to talk or shake hands or acknowledge the crowds. It would throw off his concentration. This time, however, Terry stopped. It's the only time I can remember him doing so. He walked over to the driver's window and in a calm polite voice said, "They're not using me enough."

He turned and resumed his journey, having seared another moment in my memory.

In retrospect, the woman's concern was not misplaced. There was something excessive about running a marathon a day, often on busy highways in heavy traffic. She may have been a mother imagining her own child trying to do the same. Terry's own mother had tried to stop him when he first announced his plan to run across Canada.

Nor was the woman alone in urging Terry to stop his run. There were occasional editorials and media commentaries that suggested he was pushing himself way beyond the limit.

The highest profile individual to speak up was Cliff Chadderton, a highly decorated Second World War veteran who had lost his leg below the knee from a grenade. He was the chief executive officer of the War Amps of Canada. He was concerned about the damage Terry might be doing to himself and said so.

Terry's artificial leg was subject to considerable wear and tear and by the time he reached Ottawa, it was causing him significant pain. The War Amps stepped in, providing a second artificial leg as well as on going repairs. They also referred him to leading prosthetist, Armand Viau in Hull. Mr. Viau, too, suggested Terry take a few days off to let his stump heal. Terry replied as he had to other medical advisers: "If I rested every time I had a problem with the stump, I'd still be in Nova Scotia. I know my body and when I feel I need a doctor, I will."

Were we using Terry? Not at all. The run was entirely his idea. When he'd brought it to us, the Canadian Cancer Society had advised him to undertake a more modest fundraiser. There was no changing his mind. No one could coerce Terry to do something he didn't want to do or stop him from doing something he'd decided he should do. There were particular moments along the way where he'd been taken advantage of—the double-booking of events, for instance. Otherwise, he meant what he said: we weren't using him enough.

If Terry had not been in the middle of his run that day and had taken the time to have a conversation with the screaming lady, I'm quite sure I know what he would have given her versions of two quotes he'd uttered on different occasions. "I could not leave the cancer ward knowing these faces and feelings would still exist even though I would be set free from mine [referring to the other youngster in the ward]. I was determined to take myself to the limit for this cause." And: "I got satisfaction out of doing things that were difficult. It was an incredible feeling. The pain was there, but the pain didn't matter."

He never had a chance to talk with that lady. I hope she might read this, forty years on, and understand.

And those were just some of the people we met along the road on that long, challenging, rewarding day. We were all spent by its end. We drove to our hotel near Ancaster. The 1980 Ford EconoVan had one of those push-button radios. The stations had been pre-set. Darrell wanted to listen to rock-n-roll. It wasn't to Doug's taste. That's how the fight started.

I don't remember exactly how it escalated, but it went from pushing buttons to pushing each other and, as we came to a stop in the hotel parking lot, some old-fashioned rough-housing. Terry and I both yelled at them to calm down. It was over fast and I went into Dad mode, giving out stern instructions: "Terry, go to your room. Doug, go clean the van. Darrell, get in the car [he and I had to drive back to town]."

It was the only fight the boys ever had—not bad for three young guys on the road with each other 24/7—and it was over before it began. By dinner we were all laughing about it.

CHAPTER THIRTEEN

"Goodness in the World"

TERRY WAS ALWAYS FOND OF kids. It shows in every picture you see of him chatting with youngsters at a rest stop or during a reception. The photos also show wide-eyed kids running along behind Terry on the road, which is how they became my problem.

Before I joined the Marathon of Hope, Terry inadvertently had been tripped by overeager kids who got too close to him. He became wary of anyone running alongside without giving him adequate space for the running style he adapted for his artificial leg. Somehow it became my job to corral the kids to create a safe distance around him. Why me? "They won't listen to us," said Darrell and Doug. "You're the old guy."

I guess they meant I was a father. As a result, in every town we would visit I would have to gather the youngsters and explain the routine. It was summer vacation and, back then, kids spent that time out of doors, roaming freely on the streets. Every time Terry woke from his morning rest, there would be a gaggle of enthusiastic eyed-kids waiting for him. When he started running, they'd fall in behind him, some running and some on bikes, and they would often stay for the entire afternoon. They had the energy.

Often, I would take the group aside at a rest stop and patiently explain that Terry did not mind them joining him but that he had already been tripped once by accident: "You don't want to do that, right?" They would all agree and nine times out of ten, things would go smoothly. But on many days, there was that one kid who wouldn't listen. My usual tactic with the problem kids was to warn that I would get a police officer involved. That usually worked. But one day, it didn't.

There was one young boy who would not listen. I would turn my back for a second, and he would be right on Terry's tail. It finally had to run up and hold him by the back of his shirt. At each stop, I would become increasingly stern with him. He was deaf to me—almost defiant. Terry asked me to do something about the distraction.

At the next stop, I took the kid firmly by the arm and marched him to the side of the road and read him the riot act. I got right down into his face and wagged the finger of authority at him, telling him he was going to be sent home by the police. Then I spun on my heels and walked smack into a telephone pole.

I saw stars and tasted blood on my lip. I heard a couple of chuckles from those nearby and I had to laugh myself. The kid backed off, though. He wasn't going to mess with a guy crazy enough to smack his face into a pole.

Another day, traffic was slow and backed up along Highway 2 east of Brantford. There were cars pulled over to either side of the road, their passengers standing on the pavement clapping, yelling encouragement, and, as always, donating to the cause. At one particular rest stop a large, jovial First Nations member of the OPP stood in the middle of the road. As cars passed, he would look inside the vehicle. On occasion, we could see him grin and say: "Sir/Madam, you're not wearing your seat belt. You know that could be a fine, but if you'd like to donate to Terry Fox?" The relieved driver would smile and reach for a wallet. I have no idea how much the officer raised but it was fun to watch and not a single driver complained.

That same day, Darrell approached a slow-moving vehicle with collection box in hand. He was hot, tired, and sweaty, as were we all. He held the box at arms-length. The motorist looked at the box, looked at Darrell, then reached out and grabbed a bill from it. He thanked Darrell and drove on. We were too shocked to react. Darrell actually said: "Thank you!"

Some people.

Darrell continued to keep things light on the road. He'd developed a funny tic, using the word 'Bob' as an adjective, the way others might use a swear word. "Where's my bob comb?" "Who moved my bob jeans?" "Where did we park the bob van?" It went on for the entire run. When our family later got a cat, the kids named it Bob. July 15 was Darrell's eighteenth birthday, which the citizens of Brantford helped us celebrate by presenting him with a cake at a reception for Terry at City Hall.

Ron Calhoun and family met us on the road the next day, a big day for them. You'll remember that he was the national public relations volunteer chairman for the Canadian Cancer Society and the man who helped Terry map out his route and name it the Marathon of Hope. He was also instrumental in my hiring. An executive at General Motors, he had the full support of his employer, which let him set up a separate office, a makeshift national headquarters for the run, at its plant near London.

The guys stayed the night at Ron's home in Thamesford. While Terry hit the sack early, Ron's daughter Lori took Darrell for a drive around town to show him the sights. Thirty-five years later at the opening of the Terry Fox Exhibition at the Canadian Museum of History in Hull, Quebec, Lori's mom, Fran, much to her daughter's embarrassment, would tell Darrell: "It was so cute, Lori had a crush on you back then." A lot of girls did.

The evening was particularly hot and humid and Terry did not sleep well.

I left Ron's house that evening and headed to my brother Bob's house in London. Bob, the track coach and kinesiologist, had helped us when we were near Peterborough trying to source the special balm Terry used on his stump to help with chaffing. I came from a third-generation Irish Catholic family; John was my oldest brother followed by Bob and then me and my younger sister, Beth. I often fought with brother Bob, as brothers do, and he had a habit of getting me into trouble. Prime example, he flushed an orange down the toilet one day just to see what would happen. What happened? The kitchen ceiling fell in. When dad thundered, "Who did that!?" Bob pointed to me. The two of us were nevertheless close and often inseparable.

We got into an argument that night in his living room. He had organized an honour guard of fifty runners to accompany Terry and each had raised raise at least $100 (the total came to a handsome $11,000). I told Bob that the runners would also have to collect donations along the route. He was indignant, informing me that these individuals were community leaders, doctors, lawyers, professionals and there was no way they were going to collect donations. I said I didn't care if they were King Tut; they were going to collect donations. Bob said he had the London

Firefighters coming along. They'd do the collected. I asked if they would be running or in uniform. They'd be in uniform, he said. I told him Terry would leave them in his dust, it just wouldn't work. We went to bed late, slightly miffed at each other.

The next morning, we were up at five and headed for Highway 2 outside Thamesford where Terry had started already. Bob and I hardly spoke in the car.

We were waiting where the Canadian National Railroad mainline crosses the highway. Before long we could see, far off in the distance, the flashing lights of the OPP cruiser, at least a half mile away. We got out of the car to stand in the dark. The humidity hung in the air like a wet blanket. We waited in silence.

I had witnessed the scene probably seventy-five times by now so I knew what to expect. With the headlight of the cruiser lighting the way, Terry came into view, moving closer and closer. He passed us in silence. Bob and I stood there as the rear lights of the convoy slowly moved down the road. Bob didn't move and didn't say anything for about half a minute, then simply looked at me and said: "The runners will collect the money. What do we use?"

Due to the heat and the lack of sleep the night before, Terry was only able to get in a couple of miles before his break. He slept for a few hours, then put in eight more miles before stopping and driving closer to London. Just outside the city limits, he started his run into the city center at around 10 a.m. (We would cover the miles we skipped the next day.)

Paul Cox, then twenty-seven, operated a music school in a plaza on Dundas Street, which was then near the city limits of London. Around noon, his coworker, Sharon Gaskell, said: "Terry Fox is coming soon, we have to go see him."

"He's everywhere on TV," Paul demurred. "I have work to do."

Sharon insisted and Paul gave in. When they arrived, there was hardly anyone on the sidewalk. Paul paced back and forth, wondering if he should go back to the office and finish his paperwork done. But then people started to show up, as if out of nowhere. They lined the streets and before long were a huge crowd. Soon Paul could see flashing lights off in the distance. He heard distant clapping and then cheering. In a few minutes, it got louder and then louder still. As the flashing lights of the police cruiser drew closer, the crowd was roaring. A fireman in full uniform ran up behind Paul carrying a boot overflowing with cash. Paul emptied his wallet into the boot and somehow the boot tipped over and spilled its contents on the ground. He and the fireman quickly scooped up the loot and packed it down deep so it wouldn't happen again. By the time Paul turned around again, Terry was passing within feet of him.

And then he was gone.

Paul remembers having a wide grin on his face in that moment. He turned to look at Sharon who had tears running down her face. It struck Paul how Terry had elicited two completely different responses. Sharon had been overcome by deep empathy. He was responding to hope and goodness in the world.

Paul missed the first annual Terry Fox Run the next year simply because he did not realize it was happening. He has never missed one since. He would take over the chairmanship of the local run for many years and, after moving to Alberta to be closer to family, become chairman of the Calgary and Cochrane runs. Paul is another Foxer.

A short distance down Dundas Street, Bob and his crew of runners waited. As Terry ran by, he gave a short wave to the group as they all fell silently in behind. Terry picked up his pace, as always when people wanted to run with him. He would not stop to greet them until his regular water break at the next mile marker where Doug waited with the van.

At this stop, he took a longer than normal break to speak to some of the runners and firefighters and express his appreciation for their support. It also gave him a little rest because he had pushed himself.

Gord Leach was one of the fifty area runners who would escort Terry from Beck Collegiate in East London to downtown Victoria Park. As he recalls:

We waited at the school, looking east as far as we could down Dundas St, trying to catch the first glimpse of him. I saw his head first, as he came over a knoll, still a long way off. Then, I slowly saw all of him. It shocked me. Suddenly tears came to my eyes, for I guess I expected, in my ignorance to see something like a Santa Claus figure or the Queen floating along easily, smiling and waving graciously to the appreciative crowds lining Dundas Street. Instead, in the decreasing distance, with the shimmering heat smack in the middle of the road, bobbing up and down, I saw a young man in pain.

As he approached, I noticed that his face was deadly serious, set in deep concentration, his now famous 'Fox-trot,' one hop on his artificial leg for every two on the good one. looked awkward and difficult for him. The reported lack of sleep the night before after twenty-six miles in the muggy heat had taken its toll. Perspiration matted and curled his brown hair and stained the white t-shirt and gray shorts that covered his lean muscular body. His eyes looked straight ahead... always straight ahead... in spite of motorcycled police, cheering spectators, kids on bikes and the news media.

He managed a weak smile on one of his few waves as we moved off the school lawn and onto the pavement behind him.

We did run behind him and we stayed there, it was his parade, not ours. We broke ranks only to dart into the crowd with boxes for enthusiastic donors. An elderly lady with tears in her eyes pressed a $20 bill into my hand, a little boy in a baseball cap was nudged forward and shyly dropped coins into a box.

Industrial workers either lined up outside their factories with dollar bills or dropped coins from the rooftops of their buildings. Businesses and summer schools had their staff outside and presented envelopes jammed with bills.

Several well-dressed convention attendees floated more paper money from a second-storey hotel balcony. All along the route, people of all ages responded to what they saw, and reached for wallet, pocket, or purse.

What struck me most about the crowd was the emotion. You could feel it. You could hear it. And you could see it. There were shouts and handmade signs of encouragement and praise. "Atta boy Terry." "We love you, Terry." "Keep it up, Terry." "Canada loves you, Terry." And so on.

And I saw a lot of tears—from pretty office girls, from young athletes, and from seasoned, unashamed factory workers. Some people simply stood quietly in awe of this amazing young man. Others, along with their friends and co-workers, applauded loudly and enthusiastically.

To not be moved at the sight of this heroic effort was just impossible. To witness the courage of this most unusual young man defied full description, but it hit you like a Mack truck. To see someone come so far in such a gruelling task and yet have so far to go is exhausting. His incredible determination has to be an inspiration to everybody, in whatever they do.

I said I ran with Terry Fox. But one doesn't run with Terry, one follows him and is influenced by his leadership for a long, long time.

The turnout in London was amazing. Ron Potter, chairman of the Ontario division of the Canadian Cancer Society and another of my bosses, was also among the fifty runners trailing Terry that day, as were his sons, Chris and Tim. As we passed the Kellogg plant, workers lined the road and some were standing on top of the four-storey building throwing money down to the volunteers below. The small box Tim was using to capture donations was soon filled. Someone handed him an empty pizza box and in a matter of blocks, he'd filled it, too.

We continued on down Dundas Street East, which was lined with small business and an inordinate number of somewhat seedy bars. The street was lined three and four deep, the bars and stores had all emptied out to see this kid. East London turned into downtown, the part of the city I knew best. My dad worked for many years at Ontario Furniture in the heart of London. I had spent a great deal of time in the area.

At this point, Terry was joined by seventeen-year-old Tony Coutinho who had been the Subject of *Fighting Back*, an Emmy-winning documentary about his twelve-year battle with childhood leukaemia. Tony and Terry would run the final mile side by side into the park.

I began to see familiar faces in the crowd. I could hear some folks yelling my name but I had to keep moving. At one point, I heard a voice I recognized—it was my best friend from St. Thomas, Bob McCaig, and his wife, Mary. Our kids were the same age and until I moved to Welland, he and I were inseparable. He is a successful businessman and I was a city council member and manager of the Chamber of Commerce. We worked together on many civic endeavours. I was so happy that they were able share even ten seconds of the run that I was beaming with pride.

Victoria Park is a large and elegant eighteen-acre urban garden with stately old trees, a bandshell, and a World War II memorial featuring a real tank. It has hosted many memorable community events. It was packed with people when we arrived. Kids were hanging from trees. Next to the Toronto City Hall crowd, it was the largest to greet Terry on his route.

The day meant a lot to me, with my brother organizing his runners, my sister and her family in attendance, just to the right of the stage with my parents. My oldest brother, John, was far back in the crowd, caught in the crush. I stood with my family as Terry spoke. After the ceremony, he came over to meet them and make a few jokes at my expense. I'm eternally grateful for his consideration and happy that my family got to meet Terry Fox.

The long day and its thirty-degree heat had left Terry spent. He headed to the Holiday Inn nearby for a cool shower, a bite to eat, and his nap. He also needed some repair work on his running leg. The Canadian War Amps flew in British Columbia prosthetics designer Ben Speicher, who had built Terry's original running leg. He took measurements and found that Terry's stump had shrunk over the summer and the cup needed adjusting. Terry had a back-up leg but it, too, was ill fitting. Regardless, Terry ran on the backup for two or three days while Ben reconfigured and repaired the original leg.

As this was Ron Potter's home turf, he took Darrell under his wing for a few hours. He knew Darrell's favorite pastime was playing Galaga, one of the early video console games that were then taking over the arcades. Ron gave his son, Tim, and Darrell two rolls of quarters and sent them downtown to the London arcade. Ron's other son, Chris, might have gone, too, but he was playing in a band that evening. Chris, incidentally, would later star in the long-running CBC series *Heartland*, several episodes of which were directed by none other than Gail Harvey, the photographer I'd caught at the Toronto City Hall event. Small world.

Doug, meanwhile, had checked into the hotel for some much-needed alone time. We were all exhausted but glowing with pride. It had been another great day.

CHAPTER FOURTEEN

Comparing Knees

THERE WERE DOZENS OF OCCASIONS when Terry spoke about his prosthesis—people were always curious—but two stand out in my memory. The first was back on Highway 7 near the village of Madoc, Ontario, where he was interviewed for a local cable station by Peter Sutton, a twelve-year-old Boy Scout.

It was a one-of-a-kind interview, Terry leaning against a car at the side of the road, interacting with Peter and a small number of villagers. Inevitably, someone asked: "How does your leg work?" Terry straightened himself up, paused, and then waved his real leg back and forth and delivered his line: "Just like yours." It never failed.

He went on to say he'd lost five pounds since the beginning of the run and that the thigh on his amputated leg was thinner. His stump no longer fit properly in his prosthesis. The bucket was riding high, jamming into his groin and causing a fair bit of "discomfort." I think the word pain would have been more appropriate.

Terry explained to Peter the unique difficulties of running as an above-the-knee amputee. Dr. Dick Traum, whose participation in the

1976 New York Marathon had inspired Terry to run across Canada, was a below-the-knee amputee. That meant he still had a functioning knee joint and calf muscles to propel his shorter prosthesis forward on the stride. His running motion was relatively natural. No one prior to Terry had tried to run a marathon with an above-the-knee amputation. His longer prosthesis, an adaptation of a conventional walking prosthesis, used a steel knee joint that operated like a hinge. His stump was held in the device's cup by suction as well as a belt around his waist. An elastic strap ran down the front of the prosthesis to help it snap back in position quicker after he had extended it. He gave the crowd at Madoc a demonstration.

The biggest problem, Terry said, was that his artificial leg was not designed to handle the pounding of a marathon a day. It was taking a beating and so, in turn, was he. "I know they are probably working on a running leg for above the knee amputees," he said. "I think they realize they've got a fine knee for walking but have a long way to go to make one for running. Eventually I know they will have one."

In fact, while Terry was running through Hamilton, the War Amps had stepped in to ask a team at Chedoke-McMaster hospital led by, to see if it couldn't improve his device. The team was led by Guy Martel, the hospital's head of prosthetics and orthotics, and included biomedical engineer Hubert de Bruin and mechanical technologist Edwin Iler. These men met with Terry to see how they might help. They were not able to complete their project before he had ended his run but their meeting led directly to great advancements in the prosthetics used today by para-Olympians. When you look at blade devices and other high-tech prosthetics in use today, some with integrated circuits and servo motors and sensors, you realize just how far things have come since 1980.

Terry's prosthesis was terribly crude by comparison. (Can you imagine Terry on a blade? He might have doubled his mileage.)

"The hard part is to get up every day and do it, to run, every day," he told the awed crowd. "But I can't picture myself quitting so I know I will never quit." The interview is still on YouTube.

What might not be clear in retrospect is how unusual it was at the time to hear someone speak openly about a missing limb. It was deliberate, like Terry's decision to always wear shorts so that the artificial leg was exposed. He was not only raising money for a cause but changing the way people looked at amputees and, by extension, all disabled people. They're not disabled, he was saying. They may have challenges but they are able—able enough to run a marathon a day. His advocacy on behalf of all disabled people is as much a part of the Terry Fox legacy as his fundraising for cancer research.

By the time he'd run from London to St. Mary's, Ontario, prosthetics designer Ben Speicher had repaired, readjusted, and returned Terry's original running leg, giving him relief from his barely adequate back-up.

These days in Southern Ontario were a bit of a blur to all of us. We would talk about how every town looked the same: Canadian Tire, gas station, fast-food restaurant, a car dealership, a strip mall, another fast-food restaurant, another gas station, over and over again. Crowds lined the streets every day. Traffic came to a standstill. Motorists honked their horns. It was a bit monotonous, to be honest, but Terry would say that the cheers, the shouts of supports, and the funds pouring in kept him going.

I left the run for a couple of days, heading back to the office in Toronto. All these years later, I have no clue what I did there, but I was expected to show my face. Terry and the team were hosted by a lovely family in St. Mary's. There was a barbeque complete with music and it seemed the whole town came out. Terry had a good time but, unfortunately, when he excused himself to go to bed, the party continued. He got little sleep that night. We rarely accepted invitations to stay overnight in private homes from that point forward.

In Stratford, the famed British actress, Dame Maggie Smith, who was performing at the Shakespeare festival, gave Terry a kiss on both cheeks.

In New Dundee, Terry took his morning break at the home of Cancer Society Volunteer Carolyn Beck. She notified the entire neighbourhood that Terry was coming and needed two hours of quiet. Not a soul ventured out on to the street that morning. Waking his nap, Terry descended the steep stairs from the second floor. He quipped he might fall and break his artificial leg. "Then you'll have a story to tell," he smiled at Carolyn.

In Guelph, Terry was presented with a cheque for $19,000, on top of what was collected along the road. These enormous sums—which would have seemed inconceivable during his first two months of running—were now, like the crowds he was drawing, almost routine.

In Kitchener, Terry had paused to speak to some folks along the route. Eventually, he gave me the signal that it was time to go so Doug jumped in the van and I looked for Darrell, who was off in the crowd. Just as we were about to leave, a young man walked up to us carrying a guitar case. He handed it to us. "I don't have any money, but I want to give this to Terry," he said. "Maybe he can keep it or maybe you can find someone to buy and give him the money."

Before we could say no, he turned and walked into the crowd. It was a stunning gesture—someone with no money giving his most precious possession in support of Terry and his cause. I was standing there with George Carter, the district director guiding us at this time, a good-natured man, very much in tune with Terry. We were both moved and deeply impressed, and we wondered what to do. We decided to tell Terry at the next rest stop.

"We have to give it back to him," said Terry. "We can't take his guitar."

The trouble was we didn't even know the young man's name. We had no idea how to find him. On the spot, it occurred to me to call up the local radio stations. I went on the air to report this generous, heartwarming gesture and ask the public to contact the station if anyone knew the individual who'd made the donation. Before we left town, the young man had been tracked down. George drove to his house with an autographed t-shirt from Terry, a handwritten thank-you note, and the guitar.

Amid the crowds and his growing celebrity, Terry cherished moments of peace. He met a young lady named Marlene Lott in Oakville. She and her father joined us for dinner that evening after which she and Terry went for a drive together. It was a short break from the pressures of the road with someone his own age. Mr. Lott offered to put us up at their home when we passed through Georgetown in a couple of weeks. As we approached Georgetown and contacted them, I explained the problems we had encountered staying in private homes, but they assured us they lived in a quiet rural area so we accepted.

It was a lovely evening. We played basketball on the driveway. The hoop was nailed to a worn wooden garage. At one point, Terry and I were scrimmaging as Doug and Darrell looked on. I was not remotely in Terry's league, needless to say, and I was not close to his height. I remember trying to guard him, my arms stretched as high as they would go.

"Who are you actually guarding?" he teased.

"Well, I thought you," I answered as the ball swished through the net. "But obviously not."

Looking back, that was one of the halcyon moments. Everything seemed to be going smoothly—no clouds on the horizon. None that we noticed, anyway.

Having completed our loop through Southwest Ontario, we were once again about an hour's drive from downtown Toronto. On Thursday, July 23, after Terry's ten early morning miles, we headed back into the city to the Four Seasons where Terry would be the guest of honour at a luncheon with the elite of Toronto business. It was organized by Izzy Sharp, owner of the Four Seasons chain, who continued to be a fantastic supporter of the Marathon of Hope. In addition to giving us accommodations, he had pledged $2 for every mile of Terry's journey and taken out newspaper and magazine ads challenging 999 companies to do the same. His efforts would eventually raise $10 million.

Way back in New Brunswick when I'd first met up with Terry and told him Izzy was on board, I'd suggested he call to express his appreciation. Terry immediately agreed and at his noon break we headed for a payphone. Just before he dialled, he turned to me: "I'm nervous, what do I say?"

"Just say thanks and talk to him like everyone else you've met along the way," I said.

While I did not stand close to him during the conversation, I could see his anxiety and emotion as he made his very important call. As usual with Terry, it went fine.

Now, a month and a half later, he was much more accustomed to giving interviews and meeting important people but he was feeling the same old trepidation as we drove downtown. He would be talking to a whole room full of VIPs. I gave him the same advice: "They are no different than the people you spoke to in all the little towns along the way. They know what cancer is. They know what you are doing. Just speak from the heart, like you always do."

He nodded and smiled.

All the attendees at the luncheon were in expensive suits and fancy dresses. Terry was at ease in his usual outfit, the now iconic Marathon of Hope t-shirt and sweat stained shorts. (There was no formal wear for Terry—his cleanest pair of jeans were in a ball under the van's bench.) He was entirely himself and he didn't disappoint. The guests were completely silent as he told his story of getting the cancer diagnosis and his decision to do something to make a difference and set an example in the fight against cancer. He made it clear he wanted nothing for himself. All he asked was for their support to find a cure.

The only noise in the room was the sound of Terry nervously flicking a paper clip he'd found on the podium. He had the guests in the palm of his hand. When he finished, they have him an enthusiastic standing ovation. They all reacted similarly—people on street corners, people in boardrooms. That was Terry's impact.

Izzy Sharp then contributed a little more of his own brand of magic. By then we had ticked off almost all the items on the Ontario wish list Terry had given me six weeks earlier—the CN Tower visit, the Blue Jay's game, Prime Minister Trudeau, Darryl Sittler. All that we'd missed was Bobby Orr. Izzy had arranged a private suite and an early dinner for Terry to meet his biggest sports idol.

This was 1980, before Wayne Gretzky became Wayne Gretzky. At the time, Boston Bruins' legend Bobby Orr was widely considered the greatest player ever to have laced on skates. He had played twelve seasons in the National Hockey League after joining the Bruins in 1966 and he held the record for most points and assists in a single season by a defenseman. Gretzky had only played his first NHL game in 1979. Orr was in the Hockey Hall of Fame. He *ruled*.

After an initial introduction in front of a photographer and a couple of media types, Terry and Bobby sat down on the couch and started discussing their legs. This was the second memorable conversation about Terry's prosthesis.

Orr had endured over a dozen surgeries on his knees during his career. There was no arthroscopic surgery at the time; doctors had cut his knee open time and again just to see what was wrong. The scars were brutal, as was the post-surgery recovery and rehab. When Bobby lifted the pant leg of his suit, his leg looked like a road map of scars. Terry in turn explained to Bobby how his artificial leg worked. There was immediate chemistry between the two athletes. "You were the greatest hockey player in the world and if it could help you play again," said Terry, "I'd give you my good knee and still find a way to get back to Vancouver."

The dinner was all fun. It was just the five of us in the private suite. At one point, Bobby went to the washroom. While he was in there, Darrell started picking the croutons from his Caesar salad saying: "I'm going to tell grandkids I ate Bobby Orr's croutons."

I had to go one lower: "I going to tell my grandkids I heard Bobby Orr take a pee."

It was a dream come true for Terry. Bobby presented him with a cheque for $25,000, courtesy of his sponsors at Standard Brands, and then we were off, driving back up to the York Region for the night. We'd only finished ten miles on the day, but what a day it had been. It seemed like we were on top of the world.

The next morning would crash us back to reality.

CHAPTER FIFTEEN

Do It or You're Fired

I T WAS RARE FOR TERRY to sleep in and, by extension, it was rare for all of us. But sleep in he did the morning after meeting Bobby Orr.

We started the next day at 7 a.m. just west of Richmond Hill, still basking in the glow of events at the Four Seasons. My kids had joined up with the run again after spending a couple of weeks at home in Welland. We had left district director George Carter's region and were now travelling though the Oakville district of the Canadian Cancer Society. There was no sign of the new district director, which was unusual, but I didn't mind. This was the same gentleman who had scheduled an extra event for Terry when we'd crossed his patch eleven days earlier. I was still feeling bad about letting Terry down on that occasion.

Mid-morning, who shows up but the new district director. He proudly announces that he's scheduled two receptions for Terry. Again.

At first, I thought he was joking. He wasn't.

"You what?" I yelled. "Didn't we discuss this back in Oakville? Are you f—ing kidding me? Please tell me you're not serious."

He had a big smile on his face: "They'll be big. The first one is in Bradford, then Aurora. We'll raise lots of money."

I was furious. "I can tell you right now, he won't do it. You did this once—it can't happen again. Where the hell are Bradford and Aurora?"

"They're just up the road ahead," he said.

"He doesn't do 'ahead' and he sure as hell doesn't do two events in one day, you know that!"

When Terry and I had worked on the proposed schedule back in New Brunswick, I had a firm picture of the route and the timetable all the way to Toronto, but beyond that, things were loose. For July 24, the Edmunston plan, one of the artifacts I later gave to the Canadian Museum of History, simply says: "On the road." It would be up to the district directors and key volunteers to nail things down. But there were rules and Terry was adamant about them: one event per evening and no driving head. This district director could care less. He not only scheduled two events, one ahead of us, but they were thirty minutes apart, which meant an extra hour of driving time, delaying dinner and screwing up Terry's bed time. It was incredibly inconsiderate.

I used a couple of colourful words with the district director, expressing my indignation. He was an older gentleman who was always acting superior to people around him and I've never been fond of people who put on airs. "He's not going to do it," I said. "Can't you get it through your head he's running twenty-six miles a day—he needs his rest."

Then came the threat: "We'll see, I'm calling Harry."

That's Harry Rowlands, the executive director, my big boss.

I was furious with this guy—he knew exactly what he was doing—but in my head I immediately accepted blame. I was asking myself: "How did I screw up? What did I do wrong? Who didn't I communicate this to?" Especially after what happened in Oakville, I should have had my eye on this part of the schedule. How was I going to tell Terry? What could we do? If Terry refused to show up, it would reflect on him, not the district director.

I decided not to say a word until Terry's lunch break. I didn't want to mess up his head and ruin his morning.

An hour later, it's not Harry who shows up, but a messenger from Harry. He took a firm hand. I thought it was over the top and still do, but the message was plain: Terry goes to both receptions or I am off the run and my job is in jeopardy.

I'm still angry about it forty-some years later.

Terry's break was near a small roadside inn, one of the many single-storey motels we stayed in with faux wood panelling dating from the 1960s. I told Terry I'd grab something for him to eat and bring it to his room. I also told him about the two events.

"NO! I'm not doing it," he said. "How many times do I have to say 'one reception'?"

His face turned a livid red. He stormed into his room, slamming the door behind him.

There was a greasy spoon nearby. I picked up a clubhouse sandwich and fries. It came in one of those round aluminum containers.

When I walked into Terry's room, he was laying down. He quickly sat up on the side of the bed. I opened the lid of the container, handed him his lunch, and sat down on a chair by the door.

He starts asking why he wasn't aware of this situation and why I agreed to it. We'd had similar conversations before but I had never seen him this upset. I explained that it was just dumped on me a couple of hours before and that I waited until he took his break. I told him about the messenger sent from downtown and that I could be taken off the run and lose my job.

Without warning, the entire container of sandwich and fries flew past my head, crashing on the wall behind me and spilling over the floor.

There was nothing I could do but stand up, slowly pick up the contents, apologizing as I did so. He sat in silence. I didn't know what to do other than to say again that I was sorry and leave him alone. I think I asked Doug to get him another sandwich. I walked off down the road by myself, demoralized. I'd let Terry down. I knew the rules. I knew better than to trust this district director. It was my fault for not being on top of things.

When Terry later came out of his room, he did not look at me. Glemena Bettencourt, the young lady I had enlisted as a volunteer a week earlier, was with us for the day. She remembers the incident vividly: "He and Doug got in the van. As Terry got in the van on the driver's slide, he slammed the door really hard then laid rubber as he peeled out of the parking. I had no idea what was going on but I had never seen him look like that, and [Bill] looked very sad."

Terry ran the rest of his day without speaking to me. He spoke at the first reception and then drove to the second. I saw the van pull up, the sliding door open, and Terry step out. The gentleman standing next to me at the entrance extended his hand to Terry and said, "Welcome, my name is [I don't remember]. I'm the reeve. Terry said a brusque "Big deal" and walked into the hall. This had never happened before, not even remotely. I gasped inside, turned to the man and said, "I'm so very sorry, he's never done this..."

Before I could finish, he cut me off, saying with warmth and sincerity: "Don't worry, I know he did not know about this event. I'm a runner, I know what he's going through. We're just happy he's here, no one will ever know." I wish I could remember his name—a good man.

Terry was fine with the crowd, friendly, patiently talking to people. They would never know what was going on behind the scenes.

The event ended and Terry left without speaking to me. I was shattered. Instead of heading back to the hotel, I drove to my apartment in Toronto with the kids.

I did not see Terry or talk to him for two days.

I was stunned and didn't know what to do. It felt like the end.

CHAPTER SIXTEEN

"It's Not My Run Anymore"

I SPENT THE NIGHT LOOKING DOWN from my high-rise apartment in Thorncliffe Park at the bustling Don Valley Parkway, the headlights and taillights streaking through the darkness. I was in a foul mood, my mind dwelling on previous failures, my ruined marriage. Just two weeks earlier, Terry and the team had travelled through these same streets in triumph, with a police escort. Now everything had crashed.

In the morning, I went to the office to see Harry Rowlands. He was an honourable man and I knew he would listen to what I had to say. Apart from showing up on special occasions, he'd trusted me to look after things on the road. "Go see what you can do for this kid," he had said, leaving me to it.

I explained how the district director had pulled the same scheduling stunt twice despite being aware of Terry's rules. If it were to happen again, I told Harry, I needed him to back me up. In so many words, he said his hands were tied the day before: the arrangements had been made and there was no way of cancelling the second event. He indicated he would speak to the next district director who was set to take over in a few days and lay down the law.

It was some solace but I was still hurt and angry, especially because of the damage to my relationship with Terry, which meant a great deal to me. It also bothered me that I would be blamed for the double bookings and, sure enough, I took the fall in one of the many books written about Terry Fox and the Marathon of Hope in the years after.

Despite the dark voices in my head, I knew I wasn't going to give up on Terry and I knew, despite everything that had gone down, that he would not give up on me. This was not the end, just another bump on the road.

One other thing I was certain about: I would never let it happen again.

It was a relief to have the kids with me over the weekend. I figured I would spend time with them and give Terry a couple of days to cool down. Things would be better after a little break from me. I was wrong again.

The phone rang shortly after 7 a.m. on Sunday. It was Doug: "You have to come back right away. Terry's been in a horrible mood since you left. He's hardly talking to anyone. He will hardly speak to Darrell and me."

I told him I was on my way. I later learned that Terry, too, had been in a foul mood, writing in his diary: "Today was awful, listened to inspirational tape, it rained all day."

I got the kids out of bed and told them to dress fast, no time for a shower: "We have to go right now."

We made the Holiday Inn at Barrie by 9 a.m. Doug had said they stayed there the night before and that Terry was running south of there. It guessed he would return to the hotel for his morning break. I was right. As I pulled off the highway, I could see the van and as I drove into the parking lot I found his police escort and a crowd of people waiting for Terry to get up and back on the road.

The kids made a beeline to Darrell. Doug told me Terry's room number. I entered the hotel, walked down the deserted hallway and sat on the floor waiting for him to get up. I didn't have to wait long.

The door opened. He gave me a surprised look. Even before I stood up, I started apologizing again: "I'm so sorry, I messed up. I should have known what was planned."

"Bill," he said, "we're losing control of the run. It doesn't feel like it's my run anymore."

He'd said the same thing to me a few days earlier when he was directed to run through the core of a city instead of along a bypass, adding unnecessary miles to his journey. The Canadian Cancer Society had long forgotten the indifference it had shown Terry earlier in the run. It now understood that the Marathon of Hope was a money maker and a great way to push the society's brand. It felt like the organization was hijacking the run and making Terry its show pony. This time he said it with deeper emotion and more pain in his voice.

I agreed with him. I also knew there was trouble brewing in British Columbia, where some were pushing to take control of Terry's image. I was not about to dump this political intrigue on him. The daily routine was hard enough on his psyche. I promised him that I would look after him: "I give you my word—I will find us the shortest route, one reception, that's it."

I also talked to him briefly about the incident with the gentleman who greeted him in Aurora. I told him about the man's understanding response, but I added: "You have to be careful about what you say. There will be people who can't comprehend or understand the stress you're under or how difficult every day is for you. If the press thinks you have gotten an attitude, they'll take you down as fast as they put you up."

He understood. Then he said something to me and brought it all home: "Bill, I just want to go home. I want to go home as fast as I can, the shortest route you can find."

"I'll get you there," I said, and I meant it. That was the moment I realized my loyalty to Terry outweighed my loyalty to the Canadian Cancer Society.

We both started to cry. We hugged, a tight hug. There was no one in the hall to see or hear.

"Okay, no one can see us crying," I said. "You go out that door, I'll go out that one."

We were back together, just like that.

I'd learned a hard lesson and I kept my guard up for the rest of the run. I asked questions. I made sure I knew what was planned. And I started taking a tougher stance on things I knew Terry would not go for. If I felt there might be a problem ahead, I communicated it to him to make sure we were both on the same wavelength.

On the upside, Terry put in twenty-six miles on the first day I was gone, the first time in a week he'd made that distance. On the day I returned, he knocked off another twenty-six. Those miles took us to a reception in Barrie, on the shores of Lake Simcoe. Terry was given a running shirt embossed with the town name that he wore the rest of the day.

As we were running down the street in Barrie, I had looked over to see a woman standing on the sidewalk, her hair in curlers, and a hairdresser's cape over her shoulders. She had run out of the beauty parlour to catch a glimpse of Terry. It was an amusing image, and it's stuck with me over the years.

Between the Greater Toronto Area and Barrie, Terry had run on a back road. The next morning, our OPP contingent led us onto the 400, a major four-lane divided highway, heavily travelled with cottagers heading north. It was a very different environment—the highway became a parking lot with people leaving their cars to cheer Terry on, some even climbing over the median barricade to drop money into the KFC buckets we were using to take donations. It was crazy.

A couple of young people we had met in the Hamilton, including Cam Morrison and Marlene Lott, were travelling with us for a few days. Their help collecting donations and running errands was welcome. They were amiable, low maintenance and knew the routine. In a quiet moment, Terry asked my about having Marlene as part of the team. I thought he had so few opportunities to be with people his own age, other than Doug, that she'd make a positive contribution to our daily routine. He seemed relaxed with her around and it was his business who was part of the crew.

"That was a good day," Terry would write in his journal in the evening. He had been received by a very large crowd at the Rotary Aqua Theater in Orillia on the shores of beautiful Lake Couchiching. He and I were getting along as though nothing had ever happened between us. And he'd completed yet another twenty-six-mile marathon.

The next day, July 28, was Terry's birthday. It had been five years since he was initially diagnosed with cancer and had his leg amputated. What a rollercoaster his life had been in those five years, emotionally and physically.

The weather was uncooperative on that special occasion. It was atrocious weather from beginning to end, one of the worst days we had encountered in a while. It poured most of the day with a steady wind. That didn't stop the crowds from coming out and lining the roads, however. I mentioned earlier that documentarian John Simpson had been chronicling Terry's run since Nova Scotia. His usual cameraman, Scott Hamilton, was with us that day. He captured a great scene that's appeared in almost every documentary made about Terry: a small crowd standing in the rain under green garbage bags singing Happy Birthday to him as he ran by, soaked to the skin.

We were scheduled to stop for lunch at the Holiday Inn in Orillia. I decided that a little celebration was in order. We were always coming up with pranks to try to make Terry laugh and lighten his burden so I ordered two cakes. The first was a real birthday cake to be served at lunch. The second was nothing but icing and whipped cream. The idea was for Darrell to hit his brother with the fake one but as the lunch break approached, he thought better of it, gauging Terry's mood after running all morning in wind and wet weather. I came up with Plan B. I jumped in the car, drove down the road, and told Terry what Darrell had refused to do. I didn't have to say anything more.

Terry arrived at the entrance to the Holiday Inn and everyone started singing Happy Birthday. Darrell approached Terry with the fake cake. Terry accepted it with a big grin accepted and promptly threw it at Darrell. Icing and whipped cream were flying everywhere. Others stepped in to join the fun. Terry picked up a large chunk of fake cake and took aim at Scott, the cameraman. "Don't do it," yelled Scott, "this is an expensive camera!" Terry's throw, fortunately, was slightly off target.

After the fun, the party moved inside for a luncheon, the regular crew, the camera crew— everyone. On a white board behind Terry's head was a big sign: "Happy Birthday Terry from the Orillia Holiday Inn." Not finished with the pranks, Terry in the middle of lunch took a big handful of real cake, walked around the table to where I was sitting and smashed it on my head. I thought about retaliating but we were inside the restaurant's property now. I had to suck it up.

As a crowning touch, I presented Terry with a gift from the crew. It was a toilet seat, purchased from Home Hardware. Around the rim, we had all signed our names and on the lid we wrote "Happy Birthday to A Good Shit." Terry, with great glee, took the seat, opened the lid, and stuck his head through it with a big grin. Someone snapped a picture which appeared on the front page of the *Vancouver Sun* within days.

Hours after the paper hit the street, I received a call from the prim and proper vice-president of public relations from the national office of the Canadian Cancer Society. She was not amused. In her best schoolmarm voice, she told me: "This, is not the image we expect for the Canadian Cancer Society." Harrumph!

Without missing a beat, I replied: "I'll speak to him right away. I can assure you he won't do it again."

I'm pretty sure she hung up on me. All the society cared about was the society's brand, not whether or not a college-aged kid who had taken on the herculean task of running across the country was allowed to act his age once in a while.

Birthday or not, Terry put in his miles that day and afterward we checked into the Welcome Inn, a two-storey motel, now part of the Howard Johnson chain. It would be our home base for this portion of the schedule. After parking the van and cars behind the motel, everyone was busy unloading gear and heading for their rooms. Terry motioned to me. We stepped aside and he said somewhat sheepishly: "I really like everyone's company, particularly Marlene, but I am having trouble concentrating on the run. They have to go."

I grimaced and said: "Gee, when are you going to tell them."

"I'm not," he said. "You are."

I supposed that's what I'd signed up for. A little while later, I gathered everyone around and concocted a storey that head office had called and said there were too many people travelling with Terry and everyone who wasn't essential would have to leave at the end of the next day.

Needless to say, this was all met with great disappointment and offers by people to pay their own way, camp along the way—anything to stay with the Marathon of Hope. But I stuck to the story and felt like a schmuck.

At the same time, I was telling the others they had to leave, we were joined on the road by a familiar face, Big Jack Hilliard, the district director we'd met back in Eastern Ontario. He was more than welcome. Terry was very fond of him and the feeling was mutual.

That evening we had dinner at the Beaver Creek Institution in Gravenhurst, a minimum- and medium-security federal prison with a capacity of 717 inmates. Terry had been invited by the institution' inmates and staff, who'd been following Terry's run on TV and in the newspapers. Charles Stickel, the last warden of Beaver Creek, wrote of the occasion in his 2019 book *The Inside Out Prison*:

> This was no happenstance visit. Through the summer the interest of the general public had been growing but also the interest of staff and inmates inside Beaver Creek. The prison residents closely followed Terry as he faced fatigue, waking up at 4 a.m. and running by 5 a.m. so he could complete his run of 26 miles or more each day. Terry's story was a frequent topic of discussion at Beaver Creek. Inmates and staff admired his commitment and personal strength and were engaged with his struggles and progress across Canada? That evening, after some refreshment, the forestry officer decided to simply call up the Terry Fox run organizers. Terry would travel through Gravenhurst and be taken to Beaver Creek to meet the inmates and share a meal.

There was one caveat. The forestry officer had to guarantee that there would be a donation of at least $10,000 to the Marathon of Hope. The superintendent just about fell out of his chair when his employee told him what he had done. "How are you going to pay for it," he kept saying. Ten thousand dollars was big money in Gravenhurst back in 1980.

The news got out quickly. The inmates were fired up about the Beaver Creek visit of this man of determination and mission, who faced physical challenges bigger than most. With the superintendent's support and the forestry officer's encouragement, staff and inmates began fundraising activities. Forty-five inmates from Beaver Creek sought and obtained the superintendent's permission to raise funds by doing a car wash in town one weekend. Next weekend the inmates ran a barbecue in a park in Gravenhurst where they sold hamburgers, bratwurst and sauerkraut and raised $750. The forestry officer solicited support from the Ministry of Natural Resources, service clubs, and from the local towns and municipalities where inmates did volunteer work, and raised another $920. The level of interest, anticipation and fundraising continued to grow. As the forestry officer had hoped, this became a good-news story, as the community and the prison worked together to meet the $10,000 goal.

Terry was served multiple T-bone steaks as he sat in the dining hall with the inmates and officers. A large decorated cake made by kitchen stewards and inmates was on hand for all to enjoy. The writing on the cake read, "You're somebody special."

His selfless talk to the men was well received. One inmate, Bill, who was one of the toughest inmates at Beaver Creek, gave a response, sharing that he had met a lot of tough men but there

was no one as tough as Terry Fox. There was not a dry eye in
the dining hall when speeches were done. Terry was presented
with a Beaver Creek T-Shirt, which he wore to his birthday party
with 2,000 people at the Gravenhurst arena later that evening.
The cumulative total of all donations was announced as $14,000.

It was all the more impressive that they did all this—holding a car wash
and selling barbecue in Gull Lake Park—during three days of continuously
miserable weather.

That same evening, we visited the Gravenhurst Centennial Centre
where Terry was greeted by a crowd of 3,000, a live band, and the
fourth birthday cake of the day—a giant seventy pounder donated by
Gravehurst Bakery owner Peter Rebelein, who said it was the largest he'd
ever created. It seemed every service club in town had jumped on the
bandwagon: the Lions, the Rotary, the Board of Trade. When your goal
is to raise funds to cure cancer there is no competition. The Kinsmen
held a telethon that ran on cable television until 1 a.m. Nearby towns
joined in, including Bracebridge, Huntsville, and others. The area raised
over $25,000 at a conservative guess.

The Canadian Cancer Society's Ron Calhoun triumphantly presented
Terry with a brand-new leg at the event, "a spare tire to get him home."

Terry was gracious in expressing his appreciation of everyone who
had made his day special. He meant it, but his final comment was: "The
best present I could get was twenty-six more miles to get closer to home."

Two months after the birthday celebrations, I heard from John
Simpson, whose team had been filming that day. John had taped a
microphone to Terry's shirt to capture the sounds along the road.
He invited me with some urgency to visit him in his editing suite which
was near my office in Toronto. He ran the footage from that day.

It wasn't what we saw, but what we heard that disturbed us. A constant short, continual cough. Obviously, something was wrong with Terry.

We hadn't noticed it during the run. And we hadn't seen the film before this point. John had put it in the can and sent it off to a lab to be processed (this was analog rather than digital film) and he was viewing it for the first time that day in Toronto.

We looked at each other, our eyes asking why we didn't catch this sooner. We've been haunted by the footage ever since. Could we have done something if we'd noticed sooner? Could we have convinced Terry to take a break from the highway and visit a hospital for a work up? Or was it just a cold?

We'll never know but we do know what happened barely five weeks later.

CHAPTER SEVENTEEN

"He's Not Going to Do It."

MUSKOKA IS THE HEART OF Ontario's cottage country, a land of 1,600 lakes and some of the best scenery Canada has to offer. It has been drawing families north to its cabins and resorts for more than a century, originally by steamship and train, now mostly by car up Highway 400 from the Greater Toronto Area. It's a beautiful, laid-back enclave and Terry loved running through it in the summer of 1980.

Our route was along Highway 169, a two-lane road with many hills to climb and descend but far less traffic than the 400. Things were not as chaotic for us as in previous weeks but people still turned out to cheer Terry along and make donations to the cause.

The morning after Terry's birthday we slept in which felt good for all of us. He was up at 7 a.m. and on the road an hour later, leaving from the Gravenhurst Post Office, the exact location where he had finished the day before.

Someone had loaned us an older motor home that would come in handy as we headed north where there were fewer motels to accommodate us.

It was a clunker, but useful. For now, Terry used it primarily for his morning breaks—we would hide it behind the domed sheds kept by the Ontario department of transportation along the highway and gain him a few hours of quiet.

He was wearing his new leg. It chaffed and caused him a great deal of pain. His stump was bleeding and you could see the blood on his shorts. It was not the first time this had happened but the media were now with us all day long, asking questions and showing concern.

On this day, at the nine-mile mark, Terry accepted an invitation from Edna Templeton to rest at her large home on the shores of Lake Muskoka. It was private, quiet. She did his laundry while slept and also called a few nearby summer camps to invite children in the understanding that they had to remain quiet as mice. The kids arrived in groups and sat on Edna's lawn without making a peep. She would come out of the house intermittently, putting her finger to her lips to give them a silent "shush." When Terry finally awoke and stepped out onto the veranda, about 100 kids stood to applaud him. Always great with children, he was delighted and appreciative.

While he'd been sleeping, a local reporter filed a story about the blood on Terry's shorts and it blew up on the wire services. Cliff Chadderton of the War Amps was quoted saying that while he was loath to comment because he knew Terry was headstrong, prosthetics experts in Ottawa, Hamilton, and London were concerned about what he was doing to his body. These were some of the same individuals who had told Terry they were amazed at how well the stump was holding up.

Terry was perturbed by the reports. "If you hear Terry Fox is down and out, don't believe it," he said in response. "I have seen people in so much pain—the little bit of pain I am going through is nothing. They can't shut it off and I can't shut down every time I feel a little sore."

After he'd finished his twenty-six miles on the day, he added: "Not bad for a guy who's supposed to be down and out."

While all of this was going on, I drove with Darrell and the kids two and half hours ahead to Sudbury. Darrell was going to do some media interviews to drum up local interest while I was scheduled to meet with the Sudbury organizing committee.

We checked Darrell into the Caswell Hotel where he would enjoy a rare and well-deserved night off. He wasn't entirely relaxed about being away from his brother and the run but Doug was at the wheel and Big Jack Lambert had rejoined us for a few days so Terry was in good hands.

I was scheduled to meet Lou Fine and his team in Sudbury. Lou was our next district director and a man who had strongly backed the decision by the Ontario division of the Canadian Cancer Society to sign on to the Marathon of Hope back in the spring. Lou would be responsible for us from the French River Trading Post, a popular restaurant and gift shop on Highway 69, all the way to the Manitoba border.

Lou had been a travelling shoe salesman before joining the Canadian Cancer Society and it was said he knew everybody in Ontario north of Sudbury. He stood apart from the other district directors, a little rough around the edges, gruff, opinionated, and always reluctant to back down. He did not suffer fools and he was used to getting his way.

We met in a private dining room with Lou and about eight members of the Sudbury organizing committee. I'd brought along Kerry Anne and Patrick with me, assuming it was going to be a casual, friendly meeting with enthusiastic reports of what was planned for Terry when he reached Sudbury. I was wrong.

As dinner ended, the easy chitchat turned to the route Terry would take. Lou with great excitement announced his plan to have Terry make a triumphant run into the city and right up to city hall.

"Oh, please, not this again," I thought to myself, wanting to bury my face in my hands.

"No Lou," I said gently, "Terry is going to take the by-pass. When he finishes his run for the day, we'll drive to city hall."

Lou wouldn't hear of it. He raised his voice and repeated his plan: "Bill, he's running downtown. The crowds will be big we'll raise thousands. That's the plan and that's what he'll do."

I felt my insides tighten but surprised myself by staying calm, not always my style, and reiterated: "No Lou, I can tell you 100 percent he will not run downtown. That's going to add an extra five miles and you know he always starts where he finishes, so there's another five miles. I am not going to make him run ten miles out the way."

Now Lou was yelling and pounding the table as the others sat mute, unsure what to do.

"Lou, it's not going to happen," I insisted.

"I'm calling Harry Rowlands!"

"Lou, I don't care if you call the man on the moon, I've made a promise to Terry that he will take the shortest way home. We take the by-pass. People will come out to see him, I guarantee it, and we'll raise the same amount of money. I'm not going to ask him to run one foot out of the way."

Lou kept yelling and pounding the table, acting like an overgrown kid. I couldn't hold back anymore. I made the face of a six-year-old kid and mocked him in kind, singing, "He's not going to do it, he's not going to do it, na-na-na-naya, he's not going to do it."

My kids, I suspect, wanted to hide under the table as the adults behaved like they were in kindergarten. With Lou still refusing to listen, I apologized to the others around the table and spoke to them directly, explaining that we'd had problems in the past with Terry having to run out of his way, adding miles to his already long journey. I told them I had promised him it wouldn't happen again and that I wasn't going to break that promise. I stood, thanked them for dinner, and left. The kids and I returned to the Caswell Inn and headed for the pool.

I told Darrell what had gone down. He found it all humorous but was in full agreement that we had to put Terry's needs first.

Lou drove south from Sudbury early the next morning, arriving at daybreak to join us as the Marathon of Hope exited the Muskoka region. Standing by the side of the road, he saw Terry running for the first time. He turned to me, much like my brother Bob had back in London, and quietly said: "You're right, Bill. He'll take the by-pass."

There were tears in Lou's eyes.

Before he headed back to Sudbury, Lou mentioned that he wouldn't be at French River Trading post when we got there but he'd join us a couple days later. I wondered why but didn't pursue the matter.

I later found out that Lou was going for a cancer operation. He didn't want us to know about it until he'd been given his prognosis. We'd also learned that his doctor wanted him to delay joining the run for a couple of weeks. Not Lou. He sat out only four days. When he rejoined us, he was totally on board with Terry's program.

Members of the Ontario Provincial Police continued to accompany Terry every step of the way. Each one of them was deeply moved by the experience and their assistance in managing traffic and keeping Terry safe was crucial to the success of his run. Now that we were heading into the northern reaches of the province, the detachments covered larger territories and officers tended to stay with us longer, often developing closer relationships with Terry and the team. OPP Constable John Lennox was one of these and he always went the extra mile.

As we were running north up Highway 69, Const. Lennox learned that a section of the road ahead was under construction. He called the ministry of transportation and by the time Terry arrived the next morning, crews had worked overnight to pave a long section of the highway shoulder. Const. Lennox had also arranged for a road sweeper to travel a mile ahead clearing of us, clearing rubble and small debris from the pavement to ensure sure footing for Terry.

Our next major stop was a reception in the parking lot of an Esso Service station and restaurant at Parry Sound. It was a tough day for Terry—the heat and humidity had returned. He noted in his diary that evening that he had felt weary, wobbly, and close to fainting during the day but he'd never let on to us that he was struggling. He finished up six miles beyond Parry Sound, after which we took him back to town for a special meeting.

Bobby Orr, a native of Parry Sound, had called his father, Doug, asked him to host Terry and give him a couple of his important mementos. Doug invited him into his home and showed Terry all of Bobby's awards. Terry came away with Bobby's Canada Cup jersey as well as a framed picture of what in Boston Bruin lore is referred to as "The Goal." The iconic image shows Bobby flying in the air past goalie St. Louis goalie Glen Hall a split second after he scored the winning goal forty seconds into overtime to win the 1970 Stanley Cup. Terry considered these items the greatest gifts he received along the way.

There were relatively fewer towns and hamlets along Highway 69. Traffic still slowed and people still passed the donations through car windows but the pace was more relaxed. We were able to take a couple of unscheduled stops to cool off in the roadside lakes.

At Point Au Baril, at the edge of Georgian Bay, another region of Ontario's cottage country, we were invited to spend the evening at an island home fifteen minutes by boat from the highway. It belonged to Bill Ballantyne, sales manager of CKFM, the Toronto radio station where Jeremy Brown worked. Terry preferred to take some alone time so Doug, Darrell, and I made him dinner, left him in the motor home which was parked at a nearby camp ground, and headed for Bill's place.

The island cottage was beautiful, dinner was sumptuous, and I forgot when to say "enough." I had far too much to drink and 4 a.m. came way too soon. Doug and Darrell had to hold me up as we made our way down a steep path to the boat. I lost my dinner on the short bumpy ride to shore and was a mess by the time we arrived at the motor home. I slurred unending apologies to Terry, expecting him to be livid. He thought it was funny. They left me to sleep it off as Terry began his run.

It was around noon on the day that we reached the French River Trading Post that Gail Harvey, the photographer who'd fallen into my arms at Toronto City Hall, joined the crew. She had taken time from her job at United Press Canada to follow the Marathon of Hope. Wasting no time, she had her camera out immediately and fit right in with her professionalism, friendly nature, and great sense of humour.

It was a measure of Gail's good nature and skill that when she joined us for the team dinner that evening, we were all comfortable enough to allow her to take photos. Later, as we prepared to retire for the night, I noticed she had disappeared. Doug told me that Terry had agreed to let her take photos of him as he wrote in his journal and read the Canadian Atlas for what lay ahead. This was an enormous concession by Terry, who always guarded his privacy, but Gail had quickly gained his confidence.

I asked her later what they had talked about. Gail was amazed at Terry's easy-going manner. He opened up about his feeling for Marlene Lott, who had been travelling with us earlier, and even touched on how angry he'd been at the crew earlier in the day. Gail had been there to witness it.

News stories would occasionally mention Terry's mood and bursts of anger. What they missed was the context. Not to make excuses, but he was invariably provoked. The crew spent a lot of time each day at rest stops, waiting for Terry to arrive. It could get boring so we'd start joking around and, on this day, we forgot to have Terry's sliced oranges and a glass of water waiting for him. If you are running twenty-six miles a day, you have a right to expect your team to do its part and when it doesn't, you are going to say something. In your exhausted state, that something might be blunt and heated. And it was.

The motel we'd booked for the night was small and didn't have enough rooms for all of us. Gail drew the short straw and had to share quarters with me in the Ford Econoline van. I made my bed on the bench. She had to climb up into the narrow overhead compartment. Removing her jeans for the climb, she gave me a killer glare: "Don't even think about it."

I still laugh at that glare, as does she. Over the years we've both shared that tid bit with others, a definite "Don't mess with me minute".

We were up at 5 a.m., as usual, bleary-eyed and ready to start another day. Highway 69 at the time was a two-lane road that twisted between rocky cliffs and wetlands (nothing like the four-lane divided highway of today). Gail and I were in her small hatchback. She'd started shooting well before daylight and as the sun slowly rose her trained eye saw an opportunity to shoot an especially dramatic image through the morning mist.

"I can't get it, we're on the wrong side of the road," she said.

"Why don't I just drive on the other side of the road?" I suggested.

"But we'll be going against traffic."

"That's okay," I laughed. "We're with Terry."

I drove up to our OPP escort and yelled out the window, explaining what I wanted to do.

We drove ahead, Gail jumped out of the passenger's seat, threw open the hatchback, and sat hanging out the back.

When the officer signalled that there was no oncoming traffic, I drove down the wrong lane of the highway so that Gail could shoot Terry with the mist and the rising sun behind him. It was one of those magical moments in the Marathon of Hope where everything came together perfectly—like it was meant to be. I call it the Terry Fox circle of karma. Gail captured the image of Terry that we all remember and went on to win multiple awards, including a coveted National Newspaper Award. It is still the most used picture of Terry Fox globally.

Sunrise that day was sublime. Sunset, not so much. Doug looked from the driver's seat at the van's odometer and realized something was wrong. You see, the van wasn't just transportation: it was also we were tracking our mileage. Because it was used for other purposes than accompanying Terry—transporting crew back and forth to break spots and hotels—the additional mileage had to be subtracted to determine the actual mileage of the run. Doug had discovered a flow in the calculations. The half way point of the Marathon of Hope had passed a couple of days earlier without anyone noticing.

We broke the news to Terry who was furious. It was a major psychological blow. As he wrote later in his diary: "I've been running all the way from the east coast, every day, thinking about reaching that halfway point. Nothing can make up for that disappointment."

It may seem trivial now, but we weren't running across Canada on an artificial leg, putting in twenty-six miles a day in pain, heat, wind, and rain. If the halfway point was important to Terry, it was important and should not have been missed.

CHAPTER EIGHTEEN

"You Go Get 'Em, Terry!"

OPP CONSTABLE MIKE SULLIVAN, WHO was not much older than Terry and a lot of fun to be around, joined us for a couple of days around Estaire, Ontario. He had just returned from vacation when he learned that he was assigned as our escort. Towards the end of his midnight shift, he met us at the Estaire Motel at 5 a.m. He remembers watching Terry come out of the hotel: "He did not acknowledge me and I was to find out later he didn't have a very good sleep as there was a loud band playing the night he got to the motel."

Const. Sullivan met Darrell and Doug and drove behind Terry in the dark—"not really driving," he says, but "mostly applying the brake" so as not to overtake him. "I recall my lights shining on him and I was thinking how lonely it must be for him."

The next day, Const. Sullivan was back. I'll let him tell the story from here:

We departed the Hotel and arrived at the location Terry had stopped the day before. The team had a way of knowing where they had left off by leaving a bag with rocks on the side of the road. The van had pulled ahead of the bag by a few yards and I noted that Terry walked back to the spot where the bag had been left.... I saw Terry repeat this later, never taking an inch without running. I can't describe how I felt at seeing this.

Every time someone honked on the highway, Terry, in mid-stride, would acknowledge *everyone* with the sweep of his right hand which was in cadence with his running pace ... and I mean *everyone*. If you were driving past him when you honked, the wave was done so fast and you would not have seen it in your rear-view mirror.

We stopped for breakfast and went to a restaurant in a small town and I was invited to join him, just the two of us. You should have seen what he ate. I can't remember what exactly but it enough to feed a team of hungry Sudbury miners after a Saturday night of drinking.

At a break on the Sudbury by-pass, I asked him what he thought about when he was running. Terry's response was more insightful than my question. He said he only thinks of the next mile. He concentrates on where the van was ahead of him and that's what he focused on. During this break, Darrell and I got into a play fight. Darrell grabbed my hat off my head and I chased through the fields, he was fast, I was faster. I still remember the roars of laughter as this was going on. I tackled him football style and slapped the cuffs on him. We then posed for a photo along with Bill's son, Patrick.

At one point I learn the older model RV they'd been given was experiencing a problem with the septic system and it wasn't clearing up. We pulled of the road somewhere and I made a phone call to friends at the Sudbury Regional Police. A short time later they called me back and advised me to take it to a local RV centre and it would be repaired for free. Those Sudbury cops were very persuasive.

The last early morning I was with Terry and the boys was at the western edge of the Sudbury detachment area. It was a touching moment of saying goodbye and wishing them all the best. I have many great memories of my time on the OPP, but my time with Terry Fox is the most memorable and will live with me forever.

Const. Sullivan's experience was typical of the police officers assigned to the Marathon of Hope. So, too, was the response of just about anyone who was asked to help when we ran into trouble, whether it was fixing the septic system on the RV or fixing a spring in Terry's leg, which would be another surprise along the road. Not the next one, however.

The next one was our realization in Sudbury that Darrell did not have a driver's license, never mind that he'd been driving the van since New Brunswick, and my car, and Jack Lambert's car. We huddled over what to do. Lou pulled some strings and we arranged for Darrell to immediately take a driver's test. He failed. Like any eighteen-year-old, he was devastated, but he'd get another chance before long.

As we closed in on Sudbury down Highway 69, we passed an old house by the side of the road. There was nothing special about it, although, like a lot of houses we'd passed, it had clearly seen better days. Just as we passed, we noticed a man standing on the porch. He had an artificial leg. As Terry got closer, the man came down his steps towards his fence and started on the grass parallel to the road and Terry.

He ran for about twenty yards, waving his arms, his fists clenched. "You go get 'em, Terry!" he yelled. "You go get 'em."

Just like that, we were gone, leaving him behind, still waving.

It was a poignant scene and the HBO producers of *The Terry Fox Story* saw fit to include it. The great Patrick Watson—broadcaster, director, and chairman of the CBC—played the guy on the porch. Patrick's left leg was amputated above the knee after falling from a ladder as a young man. Over the years, he would serve as chairman of the Canadian Abilities Foundation and honorary chair of the Canadian Amputee Sports Association. He is credited in the film as "Peg Leg."

Against the advice of his doctor, Lou Fine joined us near Sudbury, cancer surgery be damned. At one point, he went over to have a closer look at the famous Ford Econoline van. He immediately noticed its special aroma. The van had a closet in back, only about two feet wide and barely high enough for someone to sit on a tiny bench with a hole in the middle and a plastic bowl below. This had served as the "facilities" for Doug, Darrell, and Terry since Newfoundland. The bowl was dumped after each use but the smell hung around. Lou opened a drawer below the toilet and pulled out a bunch of white pucks. "These are for your toilet," he said. "They're supposed to be *in* your toilet. They'll kill the smell."

"Oh," we said, "we wondered what those were for."

The smell, for us, was just part of the experience. We were used to it and, as Darrell would say some years later, it served a purpose, scaring others away from the vehicle. The van was Terry's space, and the stink was like a force field that protected his privacy. People would go near the van but very rarely would they step inside.

Sticking to the plan, we took the by-pass around Sudbury. Ellen Tate, who was among those cheering Terry at the side of the road that day, told the *Sudbury Star* in 2013 what it was like: "I was expecting he'd be happy to see us but he was concentrating on every step and looked very tired. It took me a while to realize in my self-centered fifteen-year-old mind how difficult it must be. It was a still a very special moment for me." When Terry was finished running, we drove downtown where the big crowds were waiting.

Lou's wife and daughter drove him west to catch up with us in Espanola. Lou would now play a big role in the Marathon of Hope, remaining with us to the end. He had arranged for Terry to arrive at the arena reception in a convertible, accompanied by hometown hockey hero Al Secord, who was playing for the Boston Bruins at the time. Terry did not like the idea of a convertible, feeling it was too ostentatious. He had turned down limousines in Toronto, opting for cabs. Finally, after much back and forth, Lou said: "Get in the damn car, they don't give a hoot about you, they want to see the hockey player." Terry grinned and piled in. Lou had made his point. Terry liked his style.

Ken MacQueen, a reporter for the *Ottawa Citizen* and later *Maclean's* magazine, now joined the run for three days:

I flew in from Ottawa to Sudbury on August 5, 1980 to catch up with the Marathon of Hope. My employer, the *Ottawa Citizen*, was eager to have another look at Terry, whose popularity had grown exponentially after Ottawa and especially after his star turn in Toronto. I booked into the same motel as the run group, somewhere near Espanola, west of Sudbury. I met briefly that night with Doug Alward. He warned me the run would start at 5 a.m. and, oh, don't even think of talking to Terry at that hour.

I got a polite nod from Terry as he piled into the van to deliver him to the precise spot where the run had stopped the day before. It was dark and it was foggy. There, they met with a skittish OPP officer who was understandably worried about Terry and his little entourage running along the busy Trans-Canada in such dismal conditions. Terry was determined to press on, with or without a police escort. He'd heard these well-meaning concerns about his health and safety again and again. He was sick of it, and it showed. The discussion—okay, argument—was brief and intense.

The officer conceded, got on the radio, and called in a second cruiser. The run commenced, "bathed in the angry glow of flashing red lights," as I wrote in the next day's newspaper.

That was my introduction to Terry and to his ragtag crew, consisting of Doug, Terry's brother Darrell, and Bill Vigars. I don't know what I'd expected after the crowds and adulation in Southern Ontario but it was something more than this.

I was the only reporter along this hot, lonely stretch of highway. Their van smelled of old socks and fast food and Terry was... Terry. The Marathon of Hope was anything but slick. It was unadorned. It was honest. It was sweaty. It was beautiful.

Terry was stubborn. Terry was determined. Terry was in pain. Terry worked his ass off, gutting out every step, every mile, every day. I've never seen anyone work harder.

He drew strength from the thin crowds strung along the highway, and at gatherings at whistlestop communities along the highway. He'd speak about kids and hospitals and how this evil thing called cancer had to be beaten.

Then back to the motel to crash into sleep, and to ready for the next morning's return to the precise spot where he'd stopped the day before.

And that was it. Unadorned. Honest. Sweaty. Above all, beautiful. We were a family at that point, bonded by the road and to the road.

We lost the old motor home shortly after Sudbury. While we were grateful for it, there were too many things going wrong with it. Luckily, we were able to find motels and every town offered Terry free accommodations, sometimes including Doug, as well. The rest of us would either sleep in the van or pay for additional rooms. We rarely had to pay for a meal. The generosity of the people in these communities was overwhelming.

Near Iron Bridge, a very small town halfway between Sudbury and Sault Ste. Marie, we received a wonderful new addition to the run arranged by Ron Calhoun and the company he worked for, General Motors, with the support of the Jim Pattison Group back in Vancouver. It was a brand-new, full-size motor home. It came just on time as we were headed for a stretch of Northern Ontario where motels were few and far between. We no longer had to worry about finding Terry rest stops and accommodation.

We were out in the boonies the second night after the RV arrived. Terry wanted to sleep in it, testing it out. The rest of the team went ahead to accommodations Lou had arranged. I stayed behind for a while.

With the permission of a local farmer, we parked the RV down a long dead-end lane. I sparked up the water heater and poured Terry a bath in the small tub. While he soaked, I cooked up a couple of cans of beans and made him his favorite peanut butter and jam sandwiches for supper.

We had a deep and meaningful conversation that night, sitting for hours, just the two of us. He wanted to know about the breakdown of my marriage and why people didn't stay together. He was raised in a family where that was unthinkable; I was raised that way, as well. I tried my best to explain the circumstances.

We also talked about what was going on in the country at the time. He did not understand why some people in Quebec would want to separate from Canada, which he viewed as the greatest country in the world. Like him, I was at a loss to explain it.

The conversation was wide ranging and I asked Terry if he had any plans after the run. He knew he wanted to go back to Simon Fraser, but didn't want to think much about it. At that point, he was just taking one day at a time.

We said goodnight and I caught up with the crew. My kids were already in our room—Darrell was always good at keeping an eye on them. It was a rare and memorable evening.

Terry was still making good mileage despite running steadily for almost four months now and the fact that his artificial leg continued to cause him problems. He completed twenty miles the next day and a full twenty-six the one after that, which took us to Bruce Mines. It was there, before breakfast, that the spring in his leg broke. I have a vivid memory of the whole crew sitting in a small roadside restaurant with every table taken. I had Terry's leg up on my table, trying to pry the spring back into place with a butter knife. In the middle of the operation, I looked up and noticed the entire restaurant, including the kitchen crew, watching this unusual sight.

I was unsuccessful, but the Sault Ste. Marie radio station crew that was with us broadcast our predicament. In no time, a gentleman walked in and introduced himself as the owner of a car repair shop a short distance down the road.

"Give me that thing," he said. "I'll see what I can do."

While we all finished breakfast, he performed a miracle, returning with the leg in working order. As the saying goes, we depended on the kindness of strangers and they never let us down. We met saints up and down every highway that Terry ran.

Speaking of saints, when we were a day and a half out of Sault Ste. Marie, a man named J. J. Hillsinger came into the picture. He would play an important role in helping Terry along the route commonly called North of Superior and he would seriously reprimand me if he ever heard me refer to him as a saint. He was a successful businessman in the Soo, owner of several Kentucky Fried Chicken outlets as well as the Watertower Inn, the premier hotel in the city. It had everything Terry needed: a quite comfortable room, a hot tub to recuperate in, and a warm pool to take the weight off his shoulders.

J. J. had driven down to meet us at the French River. He introduced himself and offered his help, saying that when we got to Sault Ste. Marie he would look after us and introduce us to his contacts on the road north. He was beyond generous, offering Terry and the crew carte blanche, rooms and meals. Terry enjoyed the hot tub and the quiet of his room and the first-class food. We made the Inn our home base for four days, starting from Terry's arrival and driving back for three nights afterward. J. J. would also return to save the day for us again in about three weeks.

Once in Sault Ste. Marie, Lou arranged for Darrell to take a second driver's test. Lou explained the situation to the examiner so when Darrell showed up for the test, he was asked to exit a parking lot, drive around the block, and return. He was then told he'd passed the test. And not a moment too soon. A couple of days later, Darrell pulled a U-turn on the

Trans-Canada Highway and managed to get his front wheels into a ditch. He was stuck and the RV was blocking half the highway which quickly backed up. Luckily, there was a Terry Fox sign on the vehicle so the road rage of the stalled drivers was minimal.

I don't think we called a tow truck but I can't remember how we got the RV back on the road. We managed somehow and life rolled on. Darrell, mortally embarrassed, took a great deal of ribbing over the next few days.

Terry ran down Great Northern Road in Sault Ste. Marie to a reception at City Hall and made a typically good speech: "I'm just part of a team," he said. "I've got the easy part. All I have to do is run. Darrell, Doug and the cancer society's directors do all the hard work, making my job easy." It was similar to what he said at the Scarborough Civic Centre and consistent with Terry's commitment to being a team player but in a few days, it would come back to haunt us.

In the meantime, he was in good spirits. He had noted a couple of times in his journal how he enjoyed the company of Kerry Anne and Patrick and how they helped him relax at the end of the day. We reached Batchawana Bay three days out of Sault Ste. Marie. At the end of a twenty-two-mile day, mostly running in the rain, we stopped at a small hotel that could only accommodate Doug and Terry. The rest of us headed back to the Soo and another night at the Watertower Inn. While unloading in the Watertower parking lot, I noted that we'd arrived in three vehicles and Patrick didn't seem to be in any of them.

The response was the same from everyone I asked: "I thought he was with you."

I didn't panic but I was obviously concerned. As soon as we got inside, I call the motel at Batchawana Bay and asked to speak to Doug. It took a while to get him on the phone.

"Have you seen Patrick there," I asked.

"Yeah, Terry hid him under his bed until you guys left," he said. "They've gone fishing."

I just shook my head.

Kerry Anne had a room all to herself that night so both kids ended up happy.

CHAPTER NINETEEN

The Longest Hill

I HAVE TRAVELLED PARTS OF THE original 1980 route many times in the forty-three years since the Marathon of Hope. I can point out exactly where we stopped and where things happened. Some events seared themselves into my mind, such as a meeting with a mother who had lost a child to cancer. Others were just fragments of time, things that lightened up a day or made me sad, things that counted as successes and others I wished I could forget, but every one of them an indelible part of that glorious summer.

The one section of the route I had never retraced was the road from Sault Ste. Marie to Thunder Bay. So many crucial moments occurred along it that I decided, if I was going to write this book, I had to see it again. I set off in October 2022, along with Ian Harvey, my friend and collaborator. We shared a lot of stories and jokes while driving Highway 17 and met many people whose lives were touched by Terry and the Marathon of Hope. To this day, they talk about him with real warmth, as do we. It was good to know that Terry and his run live on in the hearts and minds of so many people—especially on this part of the route where the emotions are more fraught for me.

After Sault Ste. Marie we travelled directly north towards Wawa. It was the latter half of August and the weather already felt autumnal. It was raining more frequently and the early mornings were chilly. I drove back to the Soo to buy rain gear for the guys. We also dug the winter clothes they'd worn to Newfoundland out from under the bench in the van. You can imagine the shape they were in.

The Canadian Cancer Society was still not covering any of Terry's costs—only the salaries of the district directors and me—so I paid for the rain gear with some of the cash we'd collected along the way. That's how we were managing a range of expenses, including gas, Terry's oranges, and meals that weren't donated. It was a miniscule amount compared to what we were raising but I kept track of it. Some of the receipts, including the cab chit for shipping Terry's leg to Hamilton, wound up in Douglas Coupland's illustrated book, *Terry*. We called our record a running account and I don't think we heard it as a pun at the time. No one had asked us for an account of our expenses and Terry never asked where the funds were coming from but I kept the receipts regardless. I wanted to have the answers if anyone ever asked how much of the donated money went to overhead.

The morning after Batchawana Bay, a reporter from the *Globe & Mail* joined us. We gave him free rein, like all the other media who travelled with us, including Ken MacQueen, the *Toronto Star's* Leslie Scrivener, and Sarah Purcell of *Real People*. Things were a bit of a mess in the RV. It was raining and mud was being tracked into the vehicle. Terry wasn't around. It was just Darrell, Lou Fine, and myself. I'm not sure if Doug was around.

Darrell, ever the jokester, was on his hands and knees mopping up the mess. He was pretending to be Cinderella, scrubbing the floors while others were out dancing. He said he had to get the job done before Terry returned from the ball.

In the same spirit, Lou repeated to the reporter what Terry had said in his speech a few days before about us having the hard part—"all Terry has to do is run."

I remember the reporter as standoffish, more interested in hanging out in the warmth of the motor home than learning anything about Terry. I've never understood his motivation but his story in the paper the next day was a load of trash.

He twisted Darrell's words to portray him as a whiner, complaining that his brother was getting all the glory. He didn't relate that Darrell was doing a comedy routine, laughing as he spoke, and he failed to note what Darrell said in a more serious moment—that he didn't mind the work, it was his job, and he knew how hard Terry was working. He was just happy to be there.

None of that was in the story. It hit Darrell hard. He felt he had let his brother down and the hurt would last for years.

Lou fared even worse. The reporter quoted him on the newspaper's front page: "The society made the marathon a success, all Terry had to do was run." Again, there was no suggestion that the comment was intended tongue-in-cheek. Nor was it mentioned that Terry had made the same statement several times since the beginning of the run. Lou, too, was mortified.

We soon heard rumours that Toronto was about to fire Lou. Terry immediately stood up for him, saying that if that happened, "I quit running for the society." He would always back his crew.

Of all of us, Terry was the least upset by the fiasco, but he did tell Darrell not to talk to the press anymore. Terry himself wasn't sure whether to trust the press anymore. The words in that story had cut like a knife.

The *Globe* report caused a fury across the country. There were even death threats against Lou. Oddly enough, the phones at Canadian Cancer Society offices across the country were ringing non-stop with new donations.

Not one to miss an opportunity for a bad joke, I drove all the way back to Sault Ste. Marie and had t-shirts made for all of us. "I'M NOT LOU FINE," they all read, except Lou's, which read, "I'M LOU FINE." His had a bull's eye on the back. Gallows humour, but it broke the tension.

Laughs aside, I realize as I tell these stories that there were many times when I was angry that summer. Incidents like the *Globe* story infuriated me. I was enraged by district directors who wouldn't follow rules. I even got mad at individuals who caused problems in our daily routine. Part of my anger was a response to bad things happening but with benefit of hindsight I can see that I was also sad at what was happening in my personal life. I was disappointed in myself and felt I didn't measure up as a husband.

What Terry taught me, and what life experience taught me, is that you cannot carry that negativity and keep going. You have to let it go. There were things that made Terry angry that summer, as we've seen, yet every day on the run also brought hope and laughter. All it took was a smile on someone's face or a tear in someone's eye as we moved along the road and the clouds lifted for him. All those kids who ran behind Terry, all those kind people who lent a hand, he embraced them every day and it made for a magical time. We were blessed because we had a purpose and we were receiving constant validation of that purpose. Doing good and seeing good in other people makes it easier to let go of the negativity.

Fortunately, Terry's big brother Fred chose this moment to unexpectedly arrive on the scene with his wife, Theresa. He was using his vacation time to catch up with his little brother, a great surprise that lifted Terry's spirits in advance of one of his biggest challenges in the entire Marathon of Hope.

There is a long, steep incline on the Trans-Canada Highway called the Montreal River Hill. Truckers hate it because it's treacherous in winter and it's closed as many as a dozen times a year by bad weather, visibility issues, and accidents. That said, it's an essential passage between Sault Ste. Marie and Wawa along the shores of Lake Superior. It's also a tourist attraction with one of the most beautiful vistas along that stretch of highway. Locals had been talking about what a challenge the Montreal River Hill would be for Terry long before he approached. Terry, too, knew it was ahead.

We spent the evening of August 15 at the Twilight Resort campground at the foot of the hill. We were all relaxed and hanging out. To take Terry's mind off the next morning, or maybe just for fun, I found some fireworks and prepared to set them off at dusk. There was no sand so I wedged them between rocks, lit them, and stood back. They immediately toppled over, shooting Roman candles across the inlet towards campers on the opposite shore. I grabbed the remaining unexploded fireworks by hand and directed them at the water. Luckily there was no harm and I kept all my fingers. The other campers thought it was funny. It certainly took our minds off the hill.

Terry was psyched to get started the next morning. On yet another run back to Sault Ste. Marie, I'd had an additional t-shirt made. On the front: "Montreal River Hill Here I Come." On the back: "I've Got You Beat."

It was a long four-mile climb and there seemed to be a larger than normal crowd along the side of the road at the base of the hill as Terry set out. I drove to the top, parked on the side of the road and sat on the fender waiting.

The locals still talk about Terry's grit in taking on that hill. They also remember the t-shirt. It wasn't easy for him but it wasn't quite the challenge he expected. As he got to the top and came in view of me he yelled, "Is this it?"

"You did it, you did it, you're on the way home," I said.

He had a big grin on his face as we slapped hands. He kept on running, not bothering to stop for his break until he'd completed an extra mile. He was pumped.

After the run, when we were back in Vancouver, Terry and I were out for a drive when he asked if I wanted to see where he trained. Of course, I did. He took me to the base of Burnaby Mountain, not far from his home. He showed me Gaglardi Way, which rises 334 meters (1,100 feet) to the campus of Simon Fraser University. It is longer and steeper than Montreal River Hill. There is really no comparison. He'd run up Gaglardi Way almost daily while training for his trip. Terry had Montreal River Hill beat before he even started.

With his brother Fred and Theresa and Lou Fine accompanying Terry, I headed back to Toronto. It was almost a nine-hour drive through the state of Michigan. I needed to finally do some of the work the society had hired me for in the first place—the initial planning for a provincial meeting of publicity and fundraising volunteers unrelated to the run. We had about 100 people coming in late fall and Deborah Kirk and I had to settle the program and make all the arrangements.

I dropped the kids off at my parent's house in St. Thomas. The plan was for me to spend some time at the office before returning to pick them up and head back north. Things didn't go exactly as planned.

CHAPTER TWENTY

Whose Brand Is This Anyway?

I SHOULD MENTION SOMETHING ELSE THAT happened before I left Terry on his way from Sault Ste. Marie to Wawa. We got up that morning and were ready to go at 5 a.m., as usual. We found the starting point from the day before, which wasn't always easy. When you're in the middle of nowhere, the roadsides can all look the same and this was long before everyone had GPS on their phones. We spent some time searching for it and finally found it.

I had a short chat with our police escort, OPP officer Al Jordan who knew the routine and would be with us all the way to Wawa. The highway was bathed with the glow of headlights from the cruiser, the van, and my car. There were few other vehicles on this stretch of highway at that hour of the morning—just the occasional transport truck. I asked Terry if he was ready to roll and got an affirmative. I turned towards my car and had just passed the police cruiser when I heard a terrible sound. I knew immediately that Terry had fallen. This was far from routine.

I spun on my heels to see him lying face down, flat on the ground, and immediately thought the worst. I rushed to his side. Slowly he turned his face towards me and said with a sly grin, "That's the fastest I've seen you move since New Brunswick."

Everyone else raced towards him, as well. Unaided, he picked himself up, brushed the gravel from his hands and knee and simply said, "Let's try that again."

That was the Terry I loved: take a fall, get back on your feet, brush yourself off, and start over. "I was never impressed with a young man as I was with Terry," Al Jordan wrote later. "He was humble and so dedicated to his task."

While I was away, Terry ran through Lake Superior Park, completing another full marathon that day, his muscles sore from all the hills along Highway 17. He was thrilled to see two moose not far from the road—after covering about 3,000 miles to that point, the run was still a great adventure for him. The next day he would reach Wawa, the home of a twenty-eight-foot-tall goose statue with its twenty-two-foot wingspan. Wawa, by the way, is the Michipicoten First Nation's name for goose.

Wawa had gone all out to raise funds for Terry's cause. Their total, including what had been raised along the highway since Sault Ste. Marie, was a whopping $44,000. That wonderful news was offset for Terry and the crew by unwelcome reports from the west coast.

On Monday, August 18, renowned broadcaster Knowlton Nash introduced a story on the CBC national news as follows: "He didn't plan on it when he set out, but it's apparent that Terry Fox has become a multi-million-dollar property, whether he likes it or not."

A BC spokesperson for the Canadian Cancer Society spokesperson was quoted as saying "that because of the incredible interest, the society cannot afford to ignore the commercial aspect of Terry's run."

Indeed, the unsmiling spokesperson spoke directly into the camera: "Up to now we haven't questioned whether it has been legitimate or not, but because there is such an influx of requests to promote different products in Terry's name, we have set up a committee. The committee will be district co-coordinators of the society as well as volunteers outside of the society who will decide what is legitimate and what isn't."

It seemed the British Columbia branch of the Canadian Cancer Society did not share Terry's core values. He had been steadfast that there would be no commercialization of his run. We'd had plenty of offers from people wanting him to endorse one thing or another. I had pulled Terry aside one day to tell him that Standard Brands, Bobby Orr's corporate sponsor, had offered to give him a new car. I'm pretty sure Bobby had no idea about this. What the company wanted in return was for their mascot, Mr. Peanut of Planter's Peanuts fame (the goober with the top hat and monocle) to run with him on his last mile through Vancouver's Stanley Park to the Pacific Ocean. Terry stared off into space, slowly rubbing his chin as though deep in thought. Then he looked at me and in just the right voice with that silly grin said, "I think that's a great idea, as long as I can wear the Mr. Peanut outfit." That tells you about his integrity and his wit. Nobody was ever going to commercialize his run. I'd told everyone I'd met at the society about his position.

The CBC's segment ended with a roadside interview with Terry from Wawa. He told it straight: "There are people back home who want me to endorse products, but I'm not going to do any of it. I think that would ruin what I am doing. I will never make any money for myself. The only thing I want to sponsor is 'Cancer Can Be Beaten.' I hope nobody tries to use me, because I won't let them."

Touché. We were obviously headed for a showdown.

I heard nothing about this while I was at the Ontario division office. By the Friday, I was ready to head north again to join the run, once again picking up the kids. The weather was lousy so we stayed overnight in St. Thomas. I visited with Mom and Dad and spent the evening at my friend Bob McCaig's home, thinking that if I left early in the morning, I should be back with the guys by mid-afternoon the next day.

At 8 p.m., the phone rang at Bob's house. It was Ron Calhoun calling from his home in London. He'd tracked me down by calling my parents. He said there was a crisis. Oh good, I thought, we haven't had one of those for at least half a day. But he was serious.

Doug had called Ron to say that Terry thought he might have a broken ankle. For the past two days, he had been soaking his foot in a bucket of ice at rest breaks. The pain was getting worse, to the point where he thought it might be impossible to continue. He'd always been able to run through pain in the past and he'd demonstrated remarkable if inexplicable recuperative abilities. How he was worried and desperate. Could this be the end?

This was a pending disaster. Ron chartered a plane out of Hamilton to fly to Marathon, an aptly named town on Highway 17 west of Wawa. I was to meet him at the London airport at 11 p.m.

Bob drove me to London which, fortunately, was less than a half hour from St. Thomas. We were anxiously sitting with Ron in the deserted terminal when a twin-engine Piper Aztec taxied up. A petite woman in uniform walked over and told us our flight was good to go. Sexists that we were at the time, Ron and I assumed the woman was a flight attendant. It turned out she was the pilot. She was so tiny that she had to sit on a couple cushions to fly the plane. Her co-pilot was a larger gentleman who made her look smaller still.

It was a nice new plane with five or six seats but I don't have much of a memory for what happened in it. Fear wiped it out. The plane taxied to the end of the runway with the wind howling and rain was pelting its wings. There was intermittent lightning. Bob told me later that he thought to himself as we took off, "I'm sure glad I'm not on that plane."

Ron told me a few years later that I spent the entire flight either in the back seat in a fetal position or curled up on the floor of the plane. The weather was so bad, the pilots decided not to proceed to Marathon and land in Sault Ste. Marie instead, waiting for it clear up or at least let up. Around 4 a.m., the crew decided we could continue but instead of flying over Lake Superior chose to follow the car lights along the highway.

There were no runway lights in Marathon so we continued on to Terrace Bay. It was light out by the time we arrived but there was fog so the pilot made a couple of passes until she saw a break and touched down. We walked over to a small unattended airport, a tiny brick building locked down tight. The gates were locked to boot. We were stuck with no way out and no phone to call for help or a taxi.

Ron and I hadn't thought to dress for the weather. We had no warm clothes with us and it was frigid. We leaned against the plane's engine cowlings to keep warm while we discussed what to do. We decided to build a human pyramid—I don't know how else to explain it. The large pilot got on all fours, Ron stood on his back and I managed to climb this human ladder, get over the chain link fence with barbed wire atop it and jump to the ground. My many years hanging out at the St. Thomas YMCA gym finally came in handy.

I proceeded to run the mile and a half into town to find a telephone booth. If you had suggested I could have done this two and a half months earlier, I would have laughed along with anyone who knew me. I'd been overweight and out of shape and it never would have happened. After a summer of running along the highways and streets of Ontario, however, I was in the best shape of my life. I found a phone at an all-night gas station and called the OPP detachment. They notified the officer accompanying Terry who was with Lou Fine in Marathon. It was a 45-minute drive for them to our landing site. I ran back to the airport and let them know Terry was on his way. Darrell and Doug would stay left behind in Marathon for two days waiting to hear transpired.

The police obviously called someone because the gates were opened by the time Terry and Lou arrived. Terry got out of the car, limping badly. Ron told him they would fly back to Sault. Ste. Marie to see a doctor. This time Terry wanted to go ahead to Thunder Bay: "I'm going west, I'm not going east!"

Ron was firm. He was getting Terry to a specialist and there wasn't one available in Thunder Bay. Terry put up an argument, digging in his heels and refusing the plan. This went back and forth between him and Ron until, finally, in exasperation, Lou, Ron, myself, and police officer Reg Essa, who would form a strong bond with Terry and accompany him until the end, all said we would quit the run if he didn't go.

It was a hollow threat and Terry knew it, but he gave in.

When we arrived at the Sault Ste. Marie hospital, Terry was dressed in jeans, shirt and running shoes. No one recognized him. It wasn't long, however, before word spread that he was back in town and in the hospital. There were a lot of chefs in the kitchen now so I let Ron handle everything. What I write next was Ron's story to me on the flight back to London the next morning.

The doctor wanted to take a few x-rays of Terry's ankle as well as his lungs. Terry bristled at the latter suggestion: "The problem is in the ankle and not my lungs." He refused the additional x-rays.

The diagnosis was not a broken ankle, but severe tendonitis and inflammation of the tendon, as might have been expected after running

3,000 miles across half of a massive country in four months flat. It amazed me all over again just how far he'd come. After the examination, the doctor asked to speak to Ron privately. He felt that Terry had a bigger problem and would only vaguely discuss it. There made it plain that he felt Terry's cancer had returned.

Ron was in a dilemma and mentally fought with himself about it. Should he confront Terry with the doctor's assessment, knowing full well that it wouldn't stop him?. Ron was left with a horrible sense of foreboding. Terry was prescribed some pain pills and told to stay off his fee for a week. There was almost zero chance he'd even agree to that.

Lou, fortunately, was thinking sharp. He convinced Terry not to return to the run immediately, to check back into the Watertower Inn for a day or two and take advantage of the hot tub and pool to ease the foot.

By the time we walked out of the hospital, there was a media contingent waiting. Terry told them what the doctor said. One reporter asked Terry which ankle was bothering him. "The one I don't have," he replied.

Terry rested the rest of the day, following Lou's advice, sitting in the hot tub, chatting with other guests of the hotel who had the unique experience of hearing Terry's story in a spa setting.

That evening. Terry had a rare date with Donna Hillsinger. She was the daughter of hotel owner J. J. and the same age as Terry. After a couple of hours cleaning up her old Valiant station-wagon, she took him across the border to a restaurant in Soo, Michigan where all the diners knew who he was and stopped by to ask for autographs. Humble as always, he was surprised the Americans knew him. Donna said later they had a nice quiet time and Terry talked of home. They went to a movie and chatted about things people their age talked about. She remembered him "as such a nice guy."

When they returned a couple hours later, Lou, Ron, J. J., the pilots and I were still in the hotel dining room chatting about world affairs. Terry and Donna came in and joined us. Sitting close by were seven or eight uniformed Canadian Air Force Rescue members. We saw them looking over at Terry. Terry was also looking at them. He said he'd like to meet them. It turned out the feeling was mutual. They had a great half hour together.

Terry slept in the next morning. When he called Lou's room and asked what time they were leaving, Lou said unfortunately they had missed the only bus that day. It was a big fat fib. The buses came thru every few hours. Lou was laying a ruse to keep Terry off his feet. Sometimes a little white lie is the best medicine because it worked on this occasion.

Early the next morning, Ron and I caught the charter back to London. The plane continued on to its home base in Hamilton. A few years ago, I tried unsuccessfully to find the crew who flew us, even reaching out to couple of pilot organizations but unfortunately, I could not track them down. This is my tip of the wing to that highly competent pilot and her co-pilot—thanks, again, for everything.

About the same time, Lou and Terry boarded a Greyhound to get back towards Marathon. Several years later, Lou would tell me a story about them both looking out the bus window as it travelled through Wawa. Lou asked if Terry noticed anything different. Terry asked what he meant. Lou replied: "A couple of days ago your picture was plastered everywhere in town. Today not a sign. You should make plans for your future after the run. People have a short memory."

Terry, in turn, told Lou he planned to keep Canadians supporting cancer research. He didn't have a definitive plan but he knew that by the time he reached the Pacific Ocean, his job, at least in his mind, would not be finished.

We all know that Terry didn't make it all the way to the Pacific but we also know that he kept up his fight on behalf of cancer research to the very end and that his work continues to this day in Canada and around the world today.

CHAPTER TWENTY-ONE

The Most Inspirational Day
of His Life

WHEN I ARRIVED BACK FROM Sault Ste. Marie at my friend Bob McCaig's house. There was a message waiting for me. Good news for a change. Greg Scott, the ten-year-old amputee Terry had met in Hamilton and his parents were going to fly north to visit Terry. The Ontario Cancer Society office told them Terry was near Terrace Bay.

I picked up my own kids from their grandparents and we headed back north, rising at dawn for the twelve-hour drive through Michigan to Marathon, catching up with the crew late in the afternoon.

To our amazement, Terry had returned from his short break looking fully recharged. He ran twenty-six miles that day despite concerns about the ankle. He was relieved the injury wasn't more serious and the whole of Canada was impressed once again by his grit.

As soon as I saw Terry, I told him the happy news that his pal Greg Scott would arrive the next day along with his parents, Rod and Sharon. Terry had called Greg from Wawa the previous week. Greg's mom had fretted that her son might be too shy to hold the conversation but they spoke for half an hour. Terry extended the invitation and the Scott family started making arrangements. They thought about driving but couldn't afford the extra time. A friend reached out to Don Chabot, who worked for the city of Welland, knowing that he had a plane. Could he fly them up? Don asked his boss for some time off. The response: "It's the chance of a lifetime. Take as much time as you need." Again, the kindness of strangers.

I also let Terry know it was going to be a very busy couple of days. In addition to Greg, John Simpson and his documentary crew were with us again and Fox family friend Doug Vater from Port Coquitlam was expected shortly. So, too, was *Toronto Star* reporter Christie Blatchford and photographer Boris Spremo. It was going to be a full house.

After the fiasco with the *Globe & Mail* story, Terry was gun shy about Christie and Boris. I explained that they were with the same paper as the more professional Leslie Scrivener and that Christie was one of Canada's most respected journalists. Boris himself was an award-winning photographer. I promised to manage things so as not to interrupt his day. He was looking forward to Greg's visit.

Terry was on a roll again the next morning, knocking off the miles as though the ankle were brand new. I am sure it was still hurting but he would never say anything. By breakfast, he had completed thirteen miles, the cool northern air making the task a bit easier. As he took his morning nap, I headed out to the airport to meet the Scotts.

I arrived at a deserted terminal, the same one we had flown into five days before to take Terry to the hospital. With all that had happened, it seemed as though a month had passed. I didn't have to wait for long. The little plane circled low overhead, landed, and taxied up to the gate. As we waited for their bags, the pilot, Don, told us that he had been following the highway and that he noticed the flashing lights of the police cruiser and saw Terry running on the highway as they approached for landing.

We dropped of the family's luggage at the hotel and immediately drove out to find Terry. For the first while, Greg rode in the van with Doug while his parents and Don followed in the RV. The crew had borrowed a bike locally, and Terry suggested to Greg that he hop on it and ride alongside him. Terry marvelled at Greg's ability on the bike, saying that when he tried to ride a bike in Port Coquitlam his leg kept falling off. Greg kept pace with his hero for six miles, the two of them chatting as they went. Several times I saw Greg's face upturned, looking wide-eyed at Terry. It was obviously a very special day for the boy. My heart swelled at the bond they were forming.

By 5 p.m. we all were ready for a good feed. Terry showered and changed and we loaded up the van and cars and headed into Terrace Bay to dine at the Red Dog Inn. Greg was shy with the newspaper photographer, camera crew, and the locals who were on hand to welcome Terry when we arrived at the restaurant. Once inside, the mood was bright. There were at least a dozen of us, including the police escort, an unusually large number, especially compared to the early days.

Greg, who had lost his hair due to the chemo treatments, kept his hat on. Terry joked with him about how they'd both lost their hair and told the story of his grown back with extra curls. Terry sat to one side of Greg at the long table, with Patrick on the opposite side, Kerry Anne directly across from them. Patrick and Greg, close to the same age, quickly became friends. Terry started playing a game with Greg, trying to guess which country's flag adorned different packets of sugar.

Still feeling a bit shy, Greg said he wasn't hungry. He ordered onion rings and a strawberry shake. Terry, meanwhile, studied the menu.

He turned to me and asked, "What's Coquille St. Jacques?" With a straight face, I said it was a dish named for a Montreal Canadiens' goalie.

By the time Terry headed to the salad bar, Greg was right behind him, shyness gone. He talked about how he wanted to be a doctor when he grew up and that he was looking forward to school in the fall and finding out who his new teacher would be. Terry spoke to Greg's father, Rod, about the amputee games he had participated in. "It was nice to get together with other amputees," he said, "but there's no competitiveness to it and I'm a competitive guy." Rod nodded towards Greg: "So is he." Soon after, Greg was talking keenly about competing in those games.

It was still early when we finished dinner and warm outside so we all head to Jackfish Lake, across the highway from our motel, the Coach House, a few miles south of Terrace Bay. There was a small sandy beach. The kids wasted no time getting into the chilly water. Terry sat in the sand watching them, his artificial leg next to him. Doug and Darrell were soon trying to push one another into the water while the kids splashed wildly. Terry stood, hopped into the shallows, and plopped himself down, immersed to his waist. In no time, Kerry Anne, Greg, and Patrick were all splashing him with the chilly water. Laughter and happy squealing abounded. It was a joyous mood—just plain silly fun.

Terry told Greg it was only the second time he had been in water since his operation and that he could no longer swim. Greg showed him how he still could. When Terry hopped back to his towel on the sand and sat down next to his prosthesis, he noticed that John Simpson had surreptitiously attached a microphone to it. He started talking in a silly stilted voice, frustrating John's efforts to catch him unguarded.

It was time for Terry to dry off and get to bed. He headed up to where the van was parked, using his artificial leg as a crutch while hopping on his real leg. He turned, smiled mischievously at those still by the water's edge, turned again and pulled down one side of his shorts, mooning the gang to uproarious laughter. The swimming scene appears in all the Terry Fox documentaries, with the mooning portion edited out. But it was pure Terry.

When everyone else had gone to bed, Lou and I sat with John Simpson and his cameraman, Scott Hamilton, at a picnic table on the motel's front lawn. The owner came out to join us with a small bottle of cognac. He opened it threw away the cork: "We're not going to need this."

We sat in the fading summer night talking about the meaning of Terry's run, how it had become bigger than we could have imagined just a few months ago, and questioning how he was able to do it day after day. Once again, 4 a.m. came early.

The next day was an all-time high for all of us, especially Terry. Greg was the poster child for all those kids across Canada with cancer, the embodiment of his inspiration for the Marathon of Hope. Once again, Greg rode in the van through the morning, and in the afternoon he took his bike out and rode beside Terry for a couple hours.

The citizens of Terrace Bay and the surrounding area gave Terry an exceptional welcome that evening. The management and staff of Kimberly Clark, the town's major employer, pulled out all the stops, fundraising, painting welcome signs, hiring a band, even setting up a small stage for Terry to address the crowd. When I returned in 2022, it was heart-warming to hear all the memories folks had about his visit. Almost everyone I met had a story to tell. Mary Deschatelets, the CEO of the Terrace Bay Library, generously spent hours digging through old files to give me background for this book.

While giving his speech on the front lawn of the Red Dog Inn, Terry was overtaken with emotion as he talked about his experience with Greg over the past two days. "I had the most inspirational day of my life today," he said. "They say it takes guts and courage to run across Canada on one leg. The courage I needed to get through chemo and treatment was much greater. I'll never forget it. I'm crying now because there's somebody right here that's going through the same thing that I went through, the exact same thing, and he's only ten-years-old. Greg Scott has been with us for two days and I haven't heard one complaint. He just had his operation two months ago. I wish he could stay with us all of the way, but he has to go back to school. Even though he has to go, he will be with me every step of the way."

Rod and Sharon later talked quietly with Terry for a few minutes later. Rod told me: "Terry is Greg's hero. He's not a rock star or a sports star, he's a real-life hero and Greg knows that."

The family flew home to Welland early the next morning. Before they left, Terry asked Doug Vater if he could give Greg a new Terry Fox flag that Doug had made for fundraising purposes back home. Of course, said Doug, and Terry presented it to Greg saying, "I'll see you again soon." Don Chabot, the pilot who made the visit possible, told me when he first met Greg in Welland, he was quiet and withdrawn but on the flight home he was upbeat and bright: "Terry had given him hope."

Doug Vater stayed with us for almost a week. He was from Port Coquitlam and had met Terry and his family at a Chamber of Commerce function where Terry received an athletic award. Doug, who owned The Pantry, a local restaurant, was master of ceremonies. Impressed with Terry and the goal he had set for himself, Doug travelled to Newfoundland and Ontario to see firsthand how the run was progressing. It was much different from seeing it on television or reading about it in a newspaper. On returning home from this visit, he would meet with Blair MacKenzie, executive director of the BC division of the Canadian Cancer Society and get the green light to set up a fund-raising campaign in PoCo, as locals call Port Coquitlam. He would also meet with Betty and Rolly to get their approval. Betty said; "It's about time somebody started doing something here." Doug would then get city council's blessing and set a fundraising target of $100,000 for the end of the year. With the help of a large contingent of volunteers and the local paper, Terry's hometown would deliver big time: $250,000, or 25 percent of Terry's initial goal of $1 million. It may seem a small amount in an age of billionaires, but it was staggering at the time.

After Greg departed, Doug showed Terry a scrapbook of press clippings to give him a flavour of what was happening back home. He could not have foreseen how one particular article would cut Terry to the quick. Flipping through the pages, Terry found a piece by Doug Collins, a well-known British Columbia controversialist who wrote for a Vancouver weekly and who would later be exposed as a virulent racist. He wrote that Terry had not actually run the entire length of Canada but had driven through Quebec, missing the province completely. It was a complete fabrication and an unwarranted attack on Terry's integrity.

Terry took it as a knife through the heart. His entire run was built on transparency and he'd been careful not to skip a single step along the way, going to great lengths to mark and return to exact spots. Crushed and furious, I asked if he wanted me to get Collins on the phone. Yes.

We were a few miles from where Terry would complete his day, staying at a little roadside motel/restaurant called the Gravel River Resort, just outside Gravel River Provincial Park. A CBC crew from Winnipeg had arrived earlier in the day, with the well-known journalist John Robertson. I felt I could trust John and let him know what was going down.

The motel office/restaurant/gift shop had a small vestibule at the entrance with a pay phone. I got Collins on the line and handed the receiver to Terry. The first words out of his mouth were: "Why would you say that? Why would you write something like that? It's a total lie, you have ruined my entire run. People will read this and believe I cheated. Why!"

Terry was crying, sobbing, saying over and over again: "Why would you do this, you haven't been anywhere near me?"

I couldn't hear what was being said on the other end but I could tell Collins was backtracking. In no mood to listen, Terry kept getting angrier and angrier, not without cause. Suddenly, he slammed the phone down and punched the wall. He was inconsolable. He just stood there, his body shaking, wracked with sobs. Everyone in the building heard the ruckus and nothing I could say would calm him down. I felt helpless.

Out of nowhere, John Robertson came over, put his arm around Terry's shoulder and said quietly: "Let's go for a walk." Still with his arm around him, they headed off across the road.

John was older than me, much taller, and distinguished looking with his graying hair. He looked like the father figure Terry needed in that moment. In fact, he was the perfect person to talk Terry off the ledge. He'd been a talented amateur baseball player before becoming a legendary sports columnist, part of his long and illustrious career in journalism. He had a quiet air of experience and was someone Terry felt he could implicitly trust.

They were gone for a long time. When they returned, Terry was calmer, the heaviness gone from his shoulders, but we all knew he was still hurting. Apart from the shock of the Collins article, he had put in a full twenty-six miles that day, one of several full marathon days in a row, the ankle was starting to bother him again and his cough had become more noticeable, a constant dry cough that we thought must be a cold. He was totally spent. He headed to his room for a shower but did come back to join us for a quiet dinner. There was sadness in the air.

John told me later that he told Terry to ignore people like Collins and anyone who didn't believe in his cause. He should remind himself why he was running and who he was running for: "Those kids you met in the cancer ward, they believe in you, and that's all that matters."

I stayed in touch with John over the years and thanked him on numerous occasions for his help that day. Without him, I don't know how Terry would have found peace.

Collins retracted his story but Terry never got over it. Someone claimed that he had not run every step of the way this far across Canada, inferring that he had cheated, that the Marathon of Hope was a sham.

Never.

CHAPTER TWENTY-TWO

As Bad as It Gets

THE MORNING AFTER THE COLLINS affair, the kids and I had to fly south for my parent's fortieth wedding anniversary. We spent the early morning with Terry on the road and afterwards the kids joined him alone in the RV for breakfast. They spent an hour together, quietly talking about the summer and the upcoming school year. Kerry Anne remembers that Terry started to cry at one point. She thought it was because they were leaving, although years later wondered if he didn't know something was wrong with his health and that he might not see them again.

Before we left, Terry signed posters, one for each kid. On Kerry Anne's he wrote: "Thanks Kerry Anne for spending most of your summer with me. I really enjoyed your company and you often helped to relax and enjoy. You are a real good kid, keep in touch and we will see you again! Terry Fox."

On Patrick's he wrote: "Thank you for letting me pinch your nose. Yes, it did make me laugh and feel good and the fact that you let me do it even though it hurt is something you should be proud of not embarrassed.

I'll never forget the way you played with Greg, as if you were lifelong friends. You're also a good kid and look forward to seeing you again keep in touch. Terry Fox."

We drove two hours to Thunder Bay and hit the department store. Shorts and running shoes were fine on the road, but they wouldn't do for their grandparent's anniversary. Then we went to a movie, our first of the summer, *Smokey and the Bandit II*, with Dom DeLuise and an elephant—just the silliness we needed following the previous day's tensions. After dinner, we checked into our hotel and I suddenly realized I'd left the bag of new clothes in the theatre. I rushed back. Thankfully, some kind soul had turned in the bag, avoiding a costly mistake. I like to credit Terry's circle of karma.

The anniversary party was great, Sunday afternoon at the Knights of Columbus Hall. The priest who had presided over the wedding forty years before was present, as was the nun who had once kicked me out of school. Monday, I headed to Welland to drop the kids at their mother's home. I planned to fly back to Thunder Bay that night but I was getting along much better with my estranged wife, Chris, and decided to stay an extra night to talk things through. It crossed my mind that there was a possibility we might be able to make a go of it again.

It occurred to me that Terry had been due to reach Thunder Bay that afternoon. Before I left, I'd taken Doug aside to tell him there might be pressure to make Terry run into the city instead of along the by-pass. I thought I should check in. It was around 6 p.m.

The crew had reservations at a Holiday Inn, arranged by Lou Fine. I called the reception desk and learned that the party had not yet registered as guests, which I found odd. Next, I called the OPP detachment to ask where Terry was. No one knew. I immediately thought something was wrong.

I sat at Chris's kitchen table wondering what to do next. With trepidation, I called the Port Arthur General Hospital, told the operator who I was, and said that I was looking for Terry. I was put on hold. My stomach was flipping over and over. I now knew something was wrong.

Sitting at the table, I had a pen in my hand and a small piece of paper on which I'd been writing information and telephone numbers. "What the hell is going on!" I wrote.

Still on hold, I kept re-tracing the words, over and over again. Finally, Lou Fine came on the line, his voice that of a man in shock: "The cancer's back, Terry's got cancer. He's been admitted, they are doing tests, but they are sure. Its back."

Lou was distraught, asking what he should do. I asked if Terry's parents knew. Lou said Terry was trying to get in touch with them.

Knowing the press, I told Lou: "Don't talk to anyone. Don't go near the press. Tell the hospital to make up a story, do anything you have to do but keep it quiet. I'll be there as fast as I can."

It was September 1, some 143 days and 3,339 miles into the Marathon of Hope, just coming into Thunder Bay. Terry had felt weak and stopped, seeking refuge in the van.

Once inside, he collapsed in the van. He told Doug to take him to a hospital, changed his mind, and asked for a doctor to come to the hotel.

Lou and Darrell went to the shopping mall where Terry was expected to appear and told the crowd that Terry was ill and the event would be rescheduled for the next day.

The doctor arrived at the hotel and did a peripheral examination. He told Terry he would have to go to the hospital for x-rays to get definitive answers. I can only imagine what Terry was going through. Also, the crew. I know it was devastating for me and they were much closer.

With Terry at the Thunder Bay hospital for an initial examination, doctors waffled on the diagnosis. More physicians were called to consult. Still no answers. Terry pushed them until, finally, one of them said: "Yes, we think your cancer has returned."

Terry knew his body. At some level, he already knew it had returned. At that moment, he also knew that it was all over. The Marathon of Hope had hit a brick wall and he had an uncertain future ahead of him. It was complete devastation.

He cried for an hour and then, in true Terry fashion, decided it would just be one more challenge. He would set an example as he had always done. Gregg Scott was in the back of his mind. He wasn't going to let his protégé down.

Maybe the Marathon of Hope wasn't over, he thought. Maybe he could beat cancer again and get back out on the road, if not from that moment, at some point later. Somehow the dream would continue. Somehow, it *must* continue, with or without him. It was consistent with what he'd said throughout the summer: "I won't quit, but if something happens to me that I can't go on, others will have to keep it going."

I got from Welland to Toronto—I'm not sure how. I was at the Air Canada counter in the airport at 6 a.m., pleading with the ticket agent to put me on the next flight to Thunder Bay. She apologized. The flight was sold out.

By this time, the news that Terry was unwell had leaked. It was said he was in hospital with an undisclosed ailment. Reporters were speculating that it was his ankle again. I discretely put my Canadian Cancer Society business card on the counter and quietly told the agent I was with Terry and had been all summer. Without going into specifics, I told her the situation was critical and that I had to be on the plane. I couldn't hold back the tears. I even offered to sit in a jump seat.

She told me she would be back shortly and disappeared. Five minutes later, she returned with someone I suspect was a supervisor, ticket in hand. I was on the flight.

Meanwhile, Doug Vater had arrived back in Port Coquitlam from Ontario. He had a number of items that Terry asked him to take to his parents' home for him. He just entered the house when the phone rang. Betty answered. It was Terry. Her first words were: "What's going on, I hear you are sick?"

"No, Mom," he replied. "The cancer is back."

She dropped the phone and Rolly had to continue the conversation.

Doug immediately arranged flights to Thunder Day and drove Rolly and Betty to the Vancouver airport. I landed at almost the same time as they did and we shared a cab to the hospital, hardly saying a word.

We found Terry in a temporary admission room, where he'd been since the night before. Lou, Darrell, and Doug were waiting in the hallway.

It was fifty-year-old hospital. The hallways were two tones of faded grey, the original terrazzo floors. It may seem odd to remember such things but the moment was so emotionally fraught that all kinds of details like these were burned into my brain and will likely stay there forever.

Rolly and Betty were ushered into the room, leaving Doug, Darrell, and Lou outside with me. Eventually Darrell and Doug went into the room. After a time, Lou and I joined.

I knew what to expect, but it didn't make it any easier to hear. Terry looked at me and said: "The cancer is back. I have to go home."

I mumbled obscenities to myself and, catching myself, immediately apologized to Betty. I don't think she noticed.

Darrell, heartbroken, said: "It's not fair."

"No, Darrell," said Terry. "I'm no different than anyone else."

Years later, in an interview with Sheldon Posen at the Canadian National Archives, Doug said that Terry had believed all summer that his enlarged heart, which pre-dated the cancer, was his biggest health risk. "I think, you know, he must have known that if the cancer came back, he was dead. Don't you think? He'd studied up on it. He thought he'd beaten it, so the cancer—he did tell me before the run, 'Doug, keep this quiet, but I have, there's some heart damage, the doctor figures, just so you're aware.' I think he thought he'd beaten the cancer. Maybe he was trying to convince himself. He was willing to die out there."

Darrell, in the same interview, continued that thought, suggesting that Terry was skeptical of medical advice. There were no benchmarks for what he was going through, he said, because what he was doing hadn't been done before. Maybe he was trying to convince himself, said Darrell. Terry skipped his appointments because "he knew that if he had those visits, everyone would be telling him to stop." And he wasn't going to stop.

That afternoon in the hospital, Terry was the most positive person in the room. He'd had time to process the information and, in his own way, he'd accepted the return of the cancer.

The doctor had explained that if Terry wanted to go home, the clock was ticking. In addition to the return of the cancer, his lung had collapsed. If he did not leave within the next few hours, his lungs would fill with fluid, stranding him in Thunder Bay until he could be stabilized. To make matters worse, he would have to be flown home lying down, which meant a private charter all the way to British Columbia.

A slew of arrangements needed to be made. Lou and I thought we ought to send Darrell and Doug home right away. Some forty-three years later, I regret that. They should have stayed and gone home the next day. There was no rush for them to leave. It would have been so much better for them to have the chance to clean out the van, their home for the past few months, and pack up their memories and make a proper goodbye. If there was one major decision that we made that summer that I could undo, it would be that one.

As Terry was admitted to a room on the hospital's third floor, Lou and I went across the street to the local Canadian Cancer Society office at Amethyst House. The building was directly opposite the emergency room entrance of the hospital. We commandeered a basement office, away from prying eyes and ears and immediately went to work.

I began preparing for a media release. My first call was to an old friend Jeff Sandler, the news director at CKPR radio. We had worked together in Welland and, much to his credit, he gave me the names and numbers of other radio, TV and newspapers outlets. He told me later that he felt there was no competition when it came to Terry. I told him I couldn't give him any details yet other than that Terry was going to make an announcement to the press, it was important, and he should have someone on the ground in Thunder Bay.

Lou was trying to line up a private flight for Terry, with little success. The *Toronto Star* offered to fly him as far as Winnipeg, where he would have had to transfer to a commercial flight. That was not an option. After no success with private companies, Lou turned to the Ontario Ministry of Health. Explaining the situation and what was needed, he was transferred several times up the ladder in the organization until he was speaking with someone described as the top bureaucrat.

"Who is going to pay for this," the bureaucrat asked.

"You are," answered Lou.

"We can't possibly do that."

"Madame," said Lou in his best I'm-not-messing-around voice, "I have all the national media from across Canada standing outside my door right now. Do you want me to go out there and tell them that the Ontario government will not fly Terry Fox home?"

"One moment, sir."

Lou was put on hold. A minute later, the bureaucrat was back. "There will be a plane there in three hours," she said.

A Canadian Cancer Society volunteer appeared in the doorway and said Terry urgently needed me in his room. When I got there, he told me he wanted to go out for lunch. He hated hospital food. The doctor had given him the okay.

Rolly, Betty, and I headed downstairs with Terry and out the side emergency door to my car, parked directly across the street. We made it as far as the middle of the road when Terry buckled. Rolly and I grabbed him by either arm. Medical staff who had been standing outside the doors came running with a gurney. We loaded him on and they rushed him back into the hospital, followed by mom and dad. I looked down to see he had dropped a shoe. I picked it up, and thought to myself, for some reason, that I should hang on to it. I'm not sure where my brain was.

I headed back downstairs to rejoin Lou in planning a press conference. We initially wanted to hold it in that basement office. I hadn't been down there half an hour when somebody burst in the door to say: "Terry wants to see you as quickly as possible." I immediately thought the worst—what had happened now?

I went flying across the street and frantically pushed the elevator button. Of course, it always comes faster if you keep pushing it. Not wanting to wait, I ran up the three flights of stairs to the third floor and into his room. He was sitting nonchalantly on the side of his bed and casually asked: "Have you seen my other shoe?"

I paused. This was the emergency?

"Yeah, I've got it across the street, I was going to keep it but I guess you can have it back."

He laughed. A tiny moment of levity in the midst of a dark day.

We moved Terry across the street to an area near the basement office where we planned to hold the press conference. Watching him walk to Amethyst House and then downstairs to the basement was painful. All energy had been sapped from his body. He moved slowly, a dramatic change from even a few days prior. I could only imagine how his parents were feeling as they walked beside him. The last time they had seen him was that triumphant weekend in Toronto.

I went outside to wait for the media to arrive and also for the ambulance that would take Terry to the airport. Christie Blatchford had flown up on the *Toronto Star* jet along with a photographer. Like everyone else, she was in shock. She would write about how the beautiful boy she'd so recently seen on the highway now could hardly get up the stairs.

As the crowd of reporters and cameramen gathered, we realized there were too many of them to fit in the basement room. We decided to move the conference outside under a covered entrance. Once the media was in place, I went back down to the basement and quietly told everyone it was time to go. The hospital staff rolled Terry to the bottom of the stairs where they planned to carry him up. He would have none of that. Rising slowly, he made his own way up to the ambulance gurney just inside the doorway. The attendants then rolled him outside to where the media were waiting, mom and dad following. It was deathly quiet.

Half sitting up in the gurney, Terry began speaking. He tried, unsuccessfully, to contain his disappointment and emotions, telling the reporters that his cancer had spread to his lungs and he had to go home for treatment. Still determined, he added: "If there is any way I can get out there again and finish it, I will."

As he spoke, Rolly and Betty stood together next to him. Betty tightly held his hand, tears staining her cheeks. Rolly had a deep sadness etched on his face. Both parents had tried to discourage Terry from the beginning and they had worried every day about his safety on the busy highways. They also knew his health challenges and were particularly worried about his heart. Now their worst fears had come to fruition. I can't imagine the heartache they were feeling.

Terry would later say that the media asked a few questions but did not badger him that evening, which he appreciated. A national outpouring of emotion began as Canadians learned the news. I remember feeling numb. I had a job to do and that was to get him home, although in retrospect I think I'd shut down emotionally after my first expletive response in the hospital room.

One of the media folks in attendance was Brian Wyatt, a CKPR radio-television reporter:

> When I was assigned to the story, I remember speculation about Terry seeing a doctor. Some thought maybe there was some sort of health issue. We scrambled to get set up, and that's when the weight of the situation became much clearer. Terry was on a stretcher, outside an ambulance.
>
> Terry said the cancer had returned to his lungs and he needed to go home for more treatment. He also said he intended to come back to Thunder Bay and resume the marathon. The determination he showed and the conviction of his words just made us totally believe that was going to happen.
>
> It wasn't until later in that evening that it really dawned on me that this was the biggest story I had ever covered and that all of

the memories of the day would be forever etched in my mind.

Years after, I still refer to it as the biggest story in my career.

There's a fool in every crowd, of course, and there was one at that press conference. He asked:

"Terry, have you signed a movie deal?"

Terry looked at him as if to say: "Have you lost your mind?" Everyone else had the same reaction.

The attendants lifted Terry into the ambulance. Betty, Rolly, Christie Blatchford and I, along with Dr. Geoff Davis, who would accompany Terry back home on the flight, climbed in to join him. Mom and dad sat to either side by his head, Dr. Davis on one side, Christie and I on the other. Initially everyone was silent.

At one point, Rolly said, "This is unfair, this is so unfair."

Terry responded as he had to Darrell: "No it's not, Dad. I am no different than anyone else. I'm not special. It happens all the time to other people. I could have sat on my rear end after the operation. I could have forgotten everything I saw in the hospital but I didn't. I just wish people would realize that anything is possible if they just try, dreams are made if you try. Maybe people will see this and go wild with fundraising."

There was a long pause before he added: "Maybe people will watch me go through treatment and they'll realize what cancer is and understand why I did this."

At the airport, the ambulance drove right out onto the tarmac to the waiting plane. Lou Fine had followed us. He stood by himself, leaning on the wing of the jet, the picture of sorrow. The attendants lifted Terry out of the ambulance and rolled the gurney to the plane. Not a word with spoken. I stood with Rolly and Betty, my arms around their shoulders.

After Terry was boarded, I walked over, bent down, and put my arms around him. I told him I loved him and that I would see him soon then stepped aside so that Dr. Davis and his parents could climb in. Lou and I stood together as the doors were closed and the jet taxied out to the runway, saying nothing as we watched it take off. We were both in shock. This wasn't how it was supposed to end.

A voice behind us said: "Mr. Vigars, there is a call for you inside."

I walked into the terminal and was directed to a phone on the wall. A voice at the other end says, "Mr. Vigars, this is CBC Radio, *As It Happens*, our host Barbara Frum would like to speak to you."

I remember some of the conversation but it's mostly a blur. A portion of it is on the CBC archives site. I said: "The dream will go on. He's on his way home now with Mom and Dad. He told me in the ambulance that he wasn't shocked that the cancer had returned and he was going to go home and fight it like the last time. I never thought he would go home this way."

At that moment, the emotion and grief I'd been suppressing overwhelmed me and I found it difficult to continue. I managed to pull myself together and Barbara Frum, to her credit, walked a fine line between giving me space and gently moving the interview along. With raw pain in my voice, I told her, "He's the greatest person I have ever met. He's twenty-two and has more guts than anyone I have ever known in my life. He taught me a lot about life. It was a fantastic two and a half months I had with him. It's sad to see it end this way. He said it was a dream to him, and maybe I'm a dreamer, too, but I think it will go on. It was very emotional. He inspired the kids he passed along the road. It doesn't matter what the end result was, what matters is that you tried and whether you were a fighter."

I ended the interview by saying, "I think this is just the beginning."

I cried all night after that. I was inconsolable, drained, and lost.

CHAPTER TWENTY-THREE

The Last Steps

I DON'T REMEMBER MUCH OF THE next forty-eight hours. Lou and I took the van to the local Salvation Army Thrift Store and gave them most of the items within. A couple of weeks later I would get a call from Betty asking if I knew what happened to Terry's good jeans. She was not pleased I had given them away.

Once we had cleaned out the van and the motor home, we parked the RV at the Canadian Cancer Society office in Thunder Bay where Terry had met the media. Lou would drive the van as far as Sudbury until we figured out its eventual destination. By lunchtime, I was on the road to Toronto. The drive took a day and a half. It's a blank.

A week later, Ron Calhoun and his wife, Fran, flew to Thunder Bay to pick up the motor home and drive it back to Vancouver. Author Elaine Cougler wrote in Ron's 2019 biography that as they headed across the prairies, long lines of cars would follow, not wanting to pass. At times it felt as if they were leading a funeral procession and the only way to get people to pass was to pull over to the side of the road. One of the cars that passed had children in the backseat holding up a hastily drawn sign: "We Love You Terry."

I was in the office on a Thursday morning, at a loss of what to do or where to start. Deborah Kirk, who had held down the fort for two and a half months, told me the place had been a madhouse since Terry's announcement. Phones were ringing off the hook with people wanting to donate and sending in funds. We received a tsunami of mail.

In a matter of hours, Harry Rowlands came knocking. He asked me to go to a CTV network office down the street. A nationwide telethon in support of Terry was being hastily pulled together for Sunday, just three days away. The program would be a tribute to Terry with star-studded entertainment; the viewing audience would be asked to phone in with pledges of financial support for Terry's cause. The producers needed to know more about the man they were honouring, so I was back on the job helping Terry.

I found myself sitting in a large, dark-panelled boardroom with a long table in the centre and banks of phones to either side, with a production assistant at each bank. The place was abuzz with activity. It looked like a scene out of a movie. Producers were rattling off questions. What kind of music did Terry like? That was easy, 1950s and 1960s country music, just like his dad. What about entertainers or sports figures—who did he admire? I answered the best I could. Remember, I had only been with him for two and a half months. It would have been so much better to have had Darrell by my side. I started out throwing out names, never thinking they could actually get them: John Denver, Anne Murray, a few athletes. He hadn't talked much about any of this on the road.

Whenever I would mention a name, someone would say, "Get Anne Murray's agent on the line, or call Darryl Sittler, we need him Sunday." Meanwhile, others were on the phone saying "Gordon Pinsent will be there.

Clyde Gray, the boxer, he can make it. Paul Williams and Elton John are in town, get them on the line." I spent the rest of the day there, trying to keep up with everything going on. It was exhilarating, watching the excitement build, and it was all for Terry.

It was a small miracle that CTV was able to get all of its affiliate stations across the country to participate. At the time, it was not a single conglomerate but a loose network of privately owned stations in major markets coast to coast. The individual station owners seldom agreed on anything, but they all bought into a national telethon to help Terry make his new goal of $10 million.

At the end of my day at the offices, the executive producer asked me where I would be on Sunday. I said, probably at home watching on TV. "Would you like to go to BC to be with Terry?" he asked.

He didn't have to ask twice.

I flew to Vancouver on Saturday and headed to the Fox home in Port Coquitlam. Terry was in the hospital so for the next three nights I slept in his bedroom. It was a normal young man's domain, except there were cardboard boxes piled to the ceiling, memorabilia presented to him by well-wishers along the way. Every item given to him—whether it was a peace pipe from a First Nation's community or a child's drawing—had been packed by volunteers since St. John's and sent home to his parents. It was all there in that small bedroom. I found it strangely comforting.

On Sunday, shortly after noon, the entire Fox family went to Royal Columbian Hospital where Terry had been admitted. Lying in bed, fully dressed, he greeted me with that great smile. It was terrific to see him. It had been only a week since we had put him on that plane in Thunder Bay but I hadn't known if I'd ever seen him again. I brought small framed photos of Kerry Anne and Patrick for him, told him that they wished they could visit him and in the meantime we all wanted him to get well. He had me put the photos on his window sill where they sat for his entire stay.

Rolly and Betty were somewhere downstairs in the hospital when the telethon started. They had agreed to answer the phones for much of the evening. Darrell, Doug, and I sat with Terry in his room watching the show. It felt good to be together, even if it was in a hospital room. Terry was amazed at what he was seeing on the screen: Elton John, John Denver, Gordon Lightfoot, Darryl Sittler—the list kept growing through the evening. CTV news anchor Lloyd Robertson was the host of the program and the audience roared with delight at the revelation of each new tally on the donations board.

Terry watched from his hospital bed as his goal of raising $1 for every Canadian took a giant leap forward that evening. It was a big lift after the unspeakable disappointments of the previous week.

Darrell and Doug left for a bit to join the Rolly and Betty answering phones and chatting with the media, which left Terry and I alone in the room. I was sitting on the side of Terry's bed, both of us in good spirits. I met Alison Ince, Terry's nurse, when she entered the room to start the intravenous for his chemo treatment. While I had been a volunteer for the Canadian Cancer Society for years, I had never known anyone who had developed cancer so I knew nothing about the treatment Terry was undergoing. As the medication took hold, he slowly fell asleep, his head resting on my shoulder. I sat there for a long time so as not to wake him.

The guys were back in the room an hour or so later and the four of us watched in amazement as the show ended. The proceeds of the six-hour telethon, together with what we raised before the run came to a screeching halt in Thunder Bay, now totalled over $10 million.

I returned to the hospital Monday morning to say goodbye to Terry, telling him I hoped to be back, although I wasn't sure when, and repeating that the kids would love to visit him. He perked up and said he'd love that.

Back in Toronto, Gail Harvey and Jeremy Brown were putting together a picture book of her photos with some words from him. I told them Terry and Betty both wanted the *Star's* Leslie Scrivener to write the book about Terry's journey. Gail and Jeremy explained that theirs was a different type of publication, mostly pictures with limited text, not the definitive story. I reiterated the family's wish, but they chose to proceed. I agreed to look at the finished product before publication to ensure it was accurate, as I would for any project—I felt we all owed it to Terry to get the facts right.

The book came out and, as Gail and Jeremy said, it was not similar to what Leslie Scrivener produced at the end of 1980. Also, they took no remuneration for their efforts and contributed $50,000 to Terry's cause. Nonetheless, I was in the doghouse for working with them, although Terry never mentioned it during our conversations.

An interesting side note about the books. One day I received a call from a gentleman named Louis Mayzel, a generous philanthropist with a great deal of love in his heart. He supported a wide array of causes, most particularly the families of police officers killed in the line of duty, and he was a fan of Terry Fox. He owned a storefront on York Street in downtown Toronto which he wanted to turn into The Terry Fox Book Store. He purchased every copy he could find of the Brown/Harvey publication as well as Leslie Scriveners's book. He provided free copies to schools across Canada and kept the store open for several months. A few years later, he contributed funds for a monument recognizing Terry's run in Liberty Park, Jerusalem. It was unveiled in 1985, with Betty and Rolly in attendance.

The next few weeks at the office were a cyclone of activity as we continued to organize the big conference coming up and coordinated the aftereffects of Terry's run. We continued to be inundated with donations, most of them coming by mail. We had to hire additional staff, Stephanie Brown, Jeremy Brown's daughter, and her friend, Katharine McClew, whose entire family would eventually become bedrock supporters of Terry's legacy. Somehow, we managed.

In the first week of October, I headed west with Kerry Anne and Patrick to see Terry again. He was out the hospital, returning intermittently for treatment. By and large, he was living a normal life, even getting out sometimes with his circle of friends.

Our visit was brief, just the weekend. Terry was overjoyed to see the kids. We all headed out to a movie, Terry, Darrell, myself, and the kids, driving from Port Coquitlam clear over to the west side of Vancouver to see *Oh God, Book II* starring George Burns. It turned out to be the story of a young girl with a higher inspiration that everyone around her thinks is crazy.

I'm not sure who chose the movie was but Terry was what I would call a quietly religious person. He didn't wear it on his sleeve but he had been reading a bit of the Bible every day during his run, as I would find out later. On one occasion, Ron Calhoun asked him, "Have you thought of taking some time off on a Sunday to go to church?"

"Have you ever read the Bible?" Terry responded.

"Parts of it," said Ron.

"Well, I've read it front to back three times and I think God will be okay to wait for me until I get home to Vancouver."

After the movie, we hit a video arcade, paradise to Darrell and Patrick, before heading home. Patrick has a vivid memory of the drive back to Port Coquitlam. We were pulled up at a light and the driver next to us was rocking out, radio blaring. Terry started rocking out, too, and we all joined in. The other driver gave us the thumbs up, a big grin on his face.

On Monday, Terry returned to the hospital to continue his treatments. Before heading to the airport, the kids and I waited at the hospital as he was admitted. We all had a chance to say goodbye to him as he lay in his bed. The kids headed downstairs and I had another moment alone with him. I told him I would stay in touch but I was pretty sure I would not be returning and this would be the last time I saw him. I bent down and hugged him tightly and told him how much I loved him. I quietly said to him, "I will make it live forever." It was a promise that I have tried to keep to this day and the main reason I have written this book.

I took a moment in the hallway to get my emotions under control before joining the kids downstairs.

I called Terry often afterward to shoot the breeze. I did not follow the news reports on his health—there had been so many inaccuracies. The demand for Terry in the months after was so high that I was often invited to events, many at schools, to tell my stories about him. It was always difficult. I would invariably choke up. When I was done, the audience would often give me a standing ovation, which made me feel life a fraud. I was standing there but I knew they were applauding Terry and the stories I would tell about him. I hated the feeling and began to question my motives for doing the talks. It got so bad that I wrote Terry a long letter, looking for guidance. I don't think it ever got to him. It was probably lost in the stacks of mail that arrived at the house in PoCo. I did tell him how I was feeling on one of our calls later in the year.

He understood and with his usual clarity told me to keep on doing whatever I was doing as long as it continued to help raise funds for the cause. I've followed his advice ever since but I've never lost that feeling of being an imposter.

Recognition continued to pour in for Terry and what he had accomplished. Schools, streets, and even a mountain were named for him. He was appreciative of it all, in his own humble way. He was sincere in not wanting to be a hero and he remained uncomfortable being called one. The only time he became genuinely excited over an acknowledgement or award was when he was named the recipient of the Lou Marsh Award, presented annually to Canada's best athlete. He had always seen his run as an athletic challenge and to be recognized by the sporting world was the highest praise he could get. And he deserved it. Every professional athlete he met along the route marvelled and respected what he was doing—a marathon a day on one leg.

He had worn a sock on his artificial leg from the day he left St. John's, never changing it. By the end of the run, it was basically a rag hanging around his shoe. In December, he realized that he was never going to return to the road. The diagnosis was bleak. He removed it just before Christmas.

My kids sent letters to Terry at Christmas. In 2015, I would come across them at the opening of the Canadian Museum History exhibition, "Terry Fox: Running Into The Heart Of Canada." They were part of the interactive display which included all the correspondence sent to Terry after the run. It was fascinating. I also found a card from my mother and father and others from my niece and my sister. Kerry Anne had clipped pictures out of the Eaton's catalogue showing what she had asked Santa for Christmas and reminiscing about her time on the road. Patrick wrote about his soccer games and asked Terry to come and visit, but added, "I know you are sick and probably won't be able to."

I pulled up these two pieces of correspondence by chance at the exhibit, simply typing in the kids' names on the keyboard. When they popped up, I was standing with a few people. I was surprised and delighted at first, followed immediately by an emotional break. I went and hid in a corner for a bit.

In early 1981, HBO announced that it would produce its first feature film. It would be about the Marathon of Hope. Robert Cooper, a successful Canadian producer was overseeing the project (he would go on to become the head of HBO). The task of writing the story outline was given to John Kastner. I was asked to share my stories with his researcher who also happened to be his mother, Rose Kastner. I readily agreed.

It was the spring of 1981. John had just won the first of his four international Emmy awards for *Fighting Back*, a documentary about children with leukaemia. Rose had been his researcher and executive producer. What was particularly sad was that she had become ill. Fatally so, as it turned out. The film, to them, was a kind of talisman, a charm for her survival. They had also made a documentary together called *Four Women*, about breast cancer.

For about three weeks, I would visit Rose at her Rosedale home and tell road stories. The first time I arrived, she had a tray with a fine array of alcoholic beverages. "Would you like a drink?" I smiled and replied, "I don't have to drink to talk about Terry."

The movie came out in 1983. I was portrayed by Oscar-winning actor Robert Duval of *The Godfather* and *Apocalypse Now* fame. I was told he took the role as Bill Vigars to raise funds for his next movie, *Tender Mercies*, for which he won that Oscar. Needless to say, when I learned he was going to portray me and we subsequently met and dined with him and his producer, my head swelled. After all, it was *the* Robert Duval. I headed to a payphone after dinner and called Chris, my wife, with whom I had reconciled for a time.

"You'll never guess who is going to play me—Robert Duval!"

"Who's he?"

"The movie star! *The Godfather*!"

"Oh, the good-looking one?"

"No, that's James Caan."

"Well, maybe I'll recognized him when I see a picture."

That took the air out of my swelled head.

As exciting as it was, the process wasn't cut and dried. I resisted signing off on the film script. Eventually the co-producer, Michael Levine, a heavy-hitter Toronto lawyer and agent, called me to his office and asked how much money I wanted. I told him none. I just wanted to make sure the story was true and accurate and not embellished in any way. He gave me the script to take home and read. I signed off that afternoon.

All I got out of the film was the right to say, "Hi, I'm Bill Vigars, Robert Duval played me in *The Terry Fox Story*." Of course, that and $5 gets me a cup of coffee.

I wasn't entirely pleased with the finished product. I thought Terry came across as angry too much of the time. He had his outbursts but he was happy and smiling for the majority of the Marathon of Hope.

The HBO movie and other films helped spread Terry's story around the world, quite literally. Judith Ray, Terry's original nurse and cheerleader, was working at a remote outstation in Papua New Guinea in the spring of 1982. One day a movie was scheduled to be shown, which was a big deal given that there was no television available. "It was supposed to be a movie about coffee growing," she said, "but the wrong reel was sent in the container. Instead, it was a film made to highlight the 1981 International Year of the Disabled and it included a cameo of Terry! This was an incredible gift because I had not seen any of the run except in the newspaper photos. To see him actually running and being acknowledged helped me actually experience the reality of it all.

The audience at the movie of course couldn't understand the grief I was exhibiting so I had to tell them the story."

As the months moved on, I would speak to Terry from time to time. He would sometimes mention how the cancer treatments were taking a toll on him. On other occasions, we'd talk about the kids and what was happening in their world. I knew his condition was deteriorating—the media was reporting on it every week—but it didn't seem that bad when I was speaking to him.

By early June, our calls had stopped. Terry was spending much more time in the hospital. Harry Rowland heard from the British Columbia office of the Canadian Cancer Society that the end was near. I received this message on Friday, June 12. I waited all weekend for news. None was forthcoming.

Monday morning, I called the house, fearing the worst. Terry's grandmother, Marian, answered and I asked to speak to Betty. She was out so I asked for Rolly. He was out with Betty. Then she said: "Do you want to talk to Terry?"

It was a complete surprise but I could hear him hop across the living room and, in my mind, I could see him. This time, we had a pretty straightforward conversation about his situation. My first words, in a tone of relief, were, "I thought you were supposed to be dying?"

"Well, I was lying in bed at the hospital and the doctor said technically, I should not be feeling as bad as I was, so I decided, I just want to go home," he replied, his voice strong.

We had a good laugh. It was my one final opportunity to speak with him. Two weeks later, I was in St. Thomas with the kids, visiting my parents. As we were leaving town, I stopped by to see my sister Beth. As I walked in her back door, she looked at me and said, "Have you heard the news?"

I didn't have to ask.

EPILOGUE

The Long Goodbye

I am not a dreamer, and I am not saying that this will initiate any kind of definitive answer or cure to cancer. But I believe in miracles. I have to.

—Terry Fox, October 1979

One day during my visit to Port Coquitlam in October 1980, Terry and I went for a drive by ourselves. He wanted to show me around his community. I was based in Ontario and really hadn't spent a lot of time in British Columbia, although it's where I now live. As we were passing the high school track where he originally trained, he casually asked if I wanted to see where he would be buried.

I didn't think it was unusual. Many of my relatives were proud to show close friends or family members where their final resting place would be. I think both of us were realistic about his prognosis which, even in those early days, was not good.

On the way to Port Coquitlam Cemetery on Oxford Street, he told me about a spot he often went to contemplate the world, long before the run: "It's just across the road from the cemetery, I'll show you when we get there."

The cemetery is small, a beautifully tended park-like setting. There are no ornate tombstones, only footstones, simple cement slab markers. We looked around and then drove to the back of the cemetery, parked the car, pushed through a broken wire fence and some bushes, and arrived at a small patch of grass where the embankment fell off steeply to Shaughnessy Street and the Coquitlam River below. This was his special spot. The view was spectacular, with the forests of the Westwood Plateau and the Northshore Mountains in the distance. At the time, you could see all the way to the Pacific Ocean. It was private and peaceful, a wonderful place to hide from the world and contemplate the future, or maybe plan a run across Canada. We sat and talked for a bit and then went for a beer.

Terry Fox died on June 28, 1981, in the early morning hours. His nurse, Alison Ince, had been responsible for his care to the very end. As deputy director of nursing at Royal Columbian Hospital, she had the unenviable duty of announcing his passing to the world on what she remembers as an otherwise beautiful Sunday morning. Terry, she said, left us "a legacy of hope which would endure as an integral part of our nation's heritage." She was right.

I spoke to Alison recently and she talked about the effect Terry had on people:

I think, partially, it was because we could all relate to him. He was our family member, friend, the guy who lived down the street and looked out for the younger kids. He was pleasant and polite to all and had an incredible pride of citizenship in Canada. Somewhat shy, he was nevertheless very determined, focused, and prepared to work hard. If there was something that he felt needed to be done, he went ahead and did it.

He had a mischievous sense of humour and loved playing pranks, but never malicious or physically hurtful ones. He was never greedy—nothing was for his benefit. He was a bright young man and was very aware of the pitfalls and problems associated with his plans for the Marathon of Hope. He had been through the fear and confronted the reality that he had cancer, would lose his leg, and his life would be changed. He knew that he needed the courage to face those changes and it had not been easy.

The description I liked best was a simple one from the late Denny Boyd, a writer for *Tri-City News* in 1980, that Terry was 'an ordinary young man who did extraordinary things.' He changed the face of cancer understanding, prevention, care, and treatment in Canada and in other parts of the world. He also changed our outlook on people who are 'differently abled' or marginalized in any way.

I wasn't able to attend Terry's funeral. We had said our goodbyes several times over the previous months and that last time I spoke to him was how I wanted to remember him. On the day it occurred, we went to the Toronto Humane Society and adopted a cat. The kids christened him Bob. Thanks Darrell—your little joke lived with them for eighteen years.

Terry's resting place, reflective of his life, is humble and unassuming, marked by a simple slab that reads: "Terrance Stanley Fox, July 28, 1958-June 28, 1981: He made his short life into a marathon of courage and hope." I've visited it several times over the years and each time there have been one or two small children's toys on the slab, left, I am sure, by a young admirer. In the midst of writing this book, I dropped by to have a chat with Terry. I left him a poppy and a Terry Fox loonie and asked his help in telling this story.

I think he came through.

Shortly after Terry's passing, young Greg Scott lost his battle with cancer. His father Rod said, "He died, unafraid, knowing that he was going to join his friend Terry."

Life went on for those of us left behind. By June 1981, Chris and I had reconciled. At the end of the school year, she and the kids moved to Toronto, a charming duplex in the Beach area, just steps from the boardwalk and Lake Ontario. The reunion lasted only eighteen months until we decided it was not meant to be. There were no lawyers, no fighting over the kids, and just a few tears. Chris moved around the corner. The arrangements were very amicable and we raised the kids jointly.

While I took joy in the fact that my family was back together, I would be lost for days in overwhelming sadness. I found comfort walking alone along the lake shore, reliving the memories of those special months. The adventure played out in my mind like a movie, vivid and clear, as it does today. It has never faded.

During its annual April Daffodil Campaign in 1983, Canadian Cancer Society volunteers encountered push back at the doorsteps. People were concerned that the society was not explaining how the funds Terry raised were being used. They weren't suggesting that anything nefarious was happening—they just wanted to know what research was being funded, where, and with what results. Thanks to Terry, people were now engaged with the idea that cancer could be beaten. They wanted answers.

I went to the National Cancer Society Office and met with the President, Dr. Robert MacBeth, a highly respected surgeon with a multi-faceted career. He quickly became irritated, particularly with me, although I was only the messenger. His frosty reply: "They don't need to know and they would not understand anyway." Volunteer Joan Gibb, who'd organized Terry's visit to Oakville and was on the national fundraising committee, also spoke up but she, too, was shut down. As a volunteer she would not suffer any repercussions. My impertinence, however, was the last straw.

A few weeks later I left the Canadian Cancer Society. It was time. It was a relief. I had become bored with the job, as usually happened in my working career when whatever I was doing ceased to challenge me. Also, with Terry gone and the legacy memorial runs in place, my work seemed complete.

Afterward, I took a number of positions in the public relations industry, including a spell at Ripley's Believe It or Not, where I made the front-page of the *Toronto Star* by stepping off the Queen Street streetcar to introduce a life-size wax figure of Pope John II to waiting media. I worked in film and television on a range of assignments including *Night Heat*, a hit CTV/CBS cop show starring Scott Hylands and Jeff Wincott that ran for four seasons. The party scene in the entertainment industry got the better of me so I moved to the West Coast for a restart and worked briefly as a chef (no previous experience) at a luxury floating fishing lodge and then as director of communications for the BC Government's Ministry of Small Business, Tourism and Culture before returning for a long stretch to the film industry.

Then came the most rewarding position of my post-Terry career. While working on *Night Heat*, I became close friends with B. J. Cook who along with Juno-award-winning musician Dominic Troiano had written the show's theme song. B. J. had been married to the legendary Grammy award-winning producer David Foster. David had established a foundation that supported families whose children required major organ transplants. B. J. suggested to him that his work could benefit from my public relations and promotional abilities. David is the real deal. He's not in it for the publicity and he truly cares about the people he is aiding. When we would visit hospitals for sick children, he would chat with each individual family, totally focused on them, as though there were no one else in the room. He refused to have the media present. I have enormous respect for him.

For two years, I travelled with David, working with my counterpart, Norm Kilarski, the fundraising chair for the organization. The business model was quite different from that of the Marathon of Hope: we put on concerts for well-heeled individuals, selling tables for ten people for anywhere from $10,000 to $50,000 with shows featuring the likes of Andrea Bocelli, Michael Bublé, Peter Cetera of Chicago, Natalie Cole, Sinbad, and Lionel Richie. I dealt with all of these entertainers and every single one treated me well. It was fun and we raised millions.

I like to think that it was Terry Fox's circle of karma that eventually led me to David Foster and the inspiring work he's undertaken. Everything I did prior to meeting Terry set me up for my relationship with the Marathon of Hope and everything I've done since has been because of Terry.

After he died, I worried that his legacy might get lost as the years passed. Yes, he'd mobilized an entire country and, yes, he'd reached his ultimate fundraising target of one dollar for every Canadian—the Marathon of Hope fund hit $24.17 million by February 1981. And it was fantastic that 300,000 people participated that year in the first annual Terry Fox Run, raising another $3.5 million. But that was in the immediate aftermath of his great achievement and his passing. I had doubts that fundraising efforts could be sustained without him.

I quit fretting with the second annual Terry Fox Run in 1983. On the Friday before the run, I was sitting on a bench by the lake across from my home in Toronto. Down the boardwalk I saw thirty or forty preschoolers walking towards me, all of them carrying their own hand-drawn sign that in one way or another said "I love Terry Fox." I realized then that Terry's marathon to find a cure for cancer would last as long as it would take. The runs continue every year on the second Sunday after Labour Day.

The first Terry Fox Run outside of Canada was organized in 1982 by journalist and runner Ed Rice in Bangor, Maine. I attended Bangor in 1984 and Betty Fox followed in 1987. Last I heard, Ed had moved to New Brunswick and is still participating in runs there.

Around the same time Ed contacted me about his Marathon of Hope, Doug Lamb and his father visited my office in Toronto. He wanted to start a Terry Fox Run at Purdue University. Forty-three years later, he is still at it, although as one of the main organizers of the Victoria run. Once you are a Foxer, you're a Foxer for life.

By 1999, according to Wikipedia, more than 1 million people ran for Terry Fox in sixty countries. By the twenty-fifth anniversary of the run, the total had grown to 3 million. Today, the Terry Fox Run is said to be the world's largest one-day fundraiser for cancer research. Close to $1 billion has been raised in his name.

One of my greatest memories is attending a Terry Fox Run in Guangzhou, China in 2015. My son Patrick is a senior administrator at the International Department of MingDe High School. He was scheduled to be the guest speaker at the annual Terry Fox Run in Guangzhou, organized by the Canadian Consul General Rachael Bedlington, but was sick and insisted I go in his place. I accompanied over 100 sixteen- and seventeen-year-old students from the school on an overnight trip. It was my first time on a bullet train. The kids, like teenagers everywhere, ran up and down the hallways until the wee hours, yet they were up at 7 a.m.

We arrived at the high-end golf course where the run was to be held and saw buses lined up for miles. As the students headed off in one direction, I was escorted to the upper level of the driving range.

I was astonished to see over 8,000 Chinese students wearing identical Terry t-shirts with Chinese lettering. Alongside them was a who's who of Guangdong province, including the governor, the mayor, and other senior political figures. It was a sight to behold. I thought of Terry—we couldn't have imagined back in 1980 having this kind of impact on the other side of the world. Incidentally, the run was sponsored by the local Four Seasons hotel thanks to Izzy Sharpe's long-time support of the Marathon of Hope. And Rachael Bedlington is now Consul General in Hong Kong-Macao where she is starting another Terry Fox Run after also seeding one in Beijing during her posting there.

I had an opportunity to speak to many of the kids at the Guangzhou run and was heartened to hear how much they knew about Terry Fox. Terry's sister Judith had been there the year before and one young man told me he was so taken by her speech he started a Terry Fox club at his school. MingDe High School students still attend Terry Fox Runs every year and Patrick uses the Marathon of Hope story as part of his teaching curriculum. I stood there thinking to myself, "We could have never imagined the impact Terry would have, not just in Canada, but around the world."

My wife, Sherry, got a firsthand taste of Terry's international appeal while visiting Cuba, which also has a successful annual run. She took a large number of Terry Tattoos, the wet-them-slap-them-on-your-arm type that kids like. At a playground full of children, she offered them as gifts. Almost instantly, the children were surrounding her, yelling Terry's name. She had to give the stack to two older students with instructions to make sure everyone got one. Curious as to how Terry became such a magical presence in Cuba, she asked around and was told that in the past, cancer had been so feared that its name was rarely spoken. His story was instrumental in bringing cancer out of the shadows as something to be fought rather than feared. That, too, is a significant part of his legacy. Judith Fox, Terry's sister, has attended the run in Cuba a couple of times. "The Cubans are very empathetic," she told me. "They love helping others and celebrate many heroes, around the world."

It's been astonishing to watch that legacy expand and to see all the amazing things that have been accomplished in his name. Shortly after Terry passed, the Ontario government announced plans to erect a monument in Thunder Bay honouring his achievement, at or close to the spot where he ended his run. The driving forces behind it were Ontario Minister of Northern Affairs Leo Bernier and Ontario Minister of Transportation James Snow. Manfred Pervich, who, as an artist, went by his first name, was commissioned.

Because of the alignment of the highway, the statue has to be placed about two-and-a-half miles from the exact spot where Terry finished. At Manfred's request, I visited his studio every few days while he was working. He would ask me questions about the curls of Terry's hair, the specific construction of the prosthesis, and other details. I was honoured to help. In appreciation, he gave me a nine-inch replica of the finished product. I believe Betty and Rolly also received one, as did Darrell and a few others, including Terry's good friend, Rick Hansen. Mine sits on a stand in our living room.

The monument was unveiled on June 26, 1982, by Governor General Edward Schreyer, who had presented the Order of Canada to Terry shortly after his run ended. In 1993, the highway was widened and the monument was moved across it. Terry now stands majestically atop a hill overlooking Lake Superior at the Thunder Bay Welcome Center. I was invited to both unveilings and returned again in October 2022 when Ian Harvey and I retraced the final portion of the journey.

I can't begin to keep up with all the memorials, buildings, institutions and events named for Terry Fox, let alone the growing number of donations. Terry is an icon in Canada and his name is everywhere, as it should be, including on his own high school: Port Coquitlam High School was renamed Terry Fox Secondary School in 1986. There are more Terry Fox statues in Thunder Bay, Ottawa, Winnipeg, and a series of four bronze sculptures by Douglas Coupland at the Terry Fox Place at BC Place in Vancouver and in his hometown of Port Coquitlam. Other buildings, theatres, a research institute, and a laboratory are named for Terry, as is a mountain in the Canadian Rockies—Mount Terry Fox, set in Terry Fox Provincial Park.

Jay Triano had the honour of unveiling the statue of Terry at SFU atop Burnaby Mountain. "After the cancer came back, he came to a game at SFU and asked me for my autograph," said Jay. "I was like, are you kidding me. You're one of Canada's greatest heroes of all time and you want my autograph? We're all inspired by different things in our lives. Sometimes it's a movie or a book you read. But to be inspired by a guy who you see work every day and know him as a friend, I feel fortunate... it was someone I actually knew. He's relevant because of the values he taught me. Find the positive when things aren't going the way you want them to go. Don't stop working. Don't stop fighting. It's helped me through everything in my life."

There's a Terry Fox Fountain of Hope on the grounds of Rideau Hall and a Canadian Coast Guard icebreaker, CCGS Terry Fox, commissioned in 1983. He's on our stamps and our dollar coin and it has been revealed that he's the first choice for our blue $5 bills. There have been songs written about him, and he's been drafted in to more Halls of Fame than most NHL hockey players. There's even a Terry Fox Hall of Fame for those who have helped improve the lives of disabled people.

In Manitoba, the province he never reached, the former civic holiday on the first Monday in August is now Terry Fox Day.

In Ontario, Terry entered the school curriculum. At some point in early 1982, I was contacted by Tom McCarthy, the principal of Pierre Laporte Junior High School in Downsview in North York. He had the idea of creating a Terry Fox study guide as a tool for teachers of such subjects as geography, history, and community service. I was honoured to be part of the project. It was a great way to remember Terry and explain our great nation.

And of course, there are the films, including two features, the 1983 *The Terry Fox Story* and CTV's 2005 *Marathon of Hope* with Shawn Ashmore (Iceman in the X-Men film series). The second movie provides a much closer portrayal of Terry. In the Duval movie, he comes across as an angry young man, which isn't how any of us knew him.

John Simpson, the film producer who was following Terry on the road in the summer of 1980, released his documentary, *I Had a Dream*, in 1981. I attended a screening with other people from the Canadian Cancer Society. John did an incredible job telling the story of Terry's journey, capturing all the emotion, pain, laughter, and challenges. When the lights came on, many in the audience were weeping.

I produced another documentary, *Terry Fox Remembered*, but the best, by far, is *Into the Wind*, produced by Victoria native and all-star NBA basketball player Steve Nash as part of ESPN's "30 for 30" series.

There will undoubtedly be more portrayals of Terry in the future. That will keep him alive in our memories. I think most people who lived through his run in 1980 still have images in their minds based on the pictures and footage of him running, his face an intense mixture of pain, concentration, and determination. My own favorite image remains his smiling face, which is why it graces the cover of this book.

To this day, I accept all invitations to speak at schools and other events about the Marathon of Hope. I'm fulfilling my promise to Terry to keep his legacy alive. It is emotionally draining at times—as was writing this book—but I do it. I tell people that Terry never wanted to be a hero; he only wanted to show he was no different than anyone else and that dreams can come true if you try. Everything he did and everything that continues to be done in his name was meant to find a cure for cancer. I never deviate from that message.

When I speak about him, I try to bring Terry alive with my words and make him real to people. He changed my life and I live with him every day. He continues to inspire countless people around the world today.

I hope this book has given you some sense of the impact he had on me and so many others. Maybe this book will inspire you to join us and continue the Marathon of Hope for as long as it takes to find that cure.

Please take a moment to visit the Terry Fox Foundation Website (https://terryfox.org/) and the Terry Fox Research Institute (https://www.tfri.ca/) and find out firsthand how Terry's Marathon of Hope has made great advances in cancer research and treatment.

ACKNOWLEDGEMENTS

I OFFER MY DEEP APPRECIATION TO my partner in this venture Ian Harvey, who has been a close friend for almost forty years. Since our first meeting when I regaled him, as I do almost everyone, with stories from my time with Terry, he has said: "You have to write a book." In recent years, his urging has become more frequent.

Between Ian, my wife Sherry, and others who pushed me to put down my memories, I realized I had to do it before it was too late. I have the Irish gift of the gab for storytelling but I am not a writer. Ian was my number-one choice to turn my stories into a book. He's smart, articulate, and a pit bull when it comes to getting things right. He also shares my sense of humor, which made him the perfect writing partner. Thank you, Ian.

This book is based on my memories from forty-three years ago. During the run I was often asked if I was taking pictures or keeping a diary. My answer was always the same: "I'm making a film in my head I will always remember." By and large that's true. The film has played over and over again in my mind all these years. That, along with the fact that I have spoken with Terry in one way or another almost every day since then, has kept my memories strong. I have made every effort to tell my recollections as accurately and honestly as possible, recognizing that memory is fallible. Where possible I have used transcripts of conversations. In some cases, I have chosen not to include individual's names, particularly in sensitive or confrontational situations as most are no longer with us to offer their side of the story.

I could not have written this memoir without the kindness of many people. Their encouragement and assistance are deeply appreciated. Thank you for your kindness as well as sharing the laughter and tears of your own memories of Terry:

Sheldon Posen, Vi and Mike Johnston, Bruno Corea, Suzanne Bourgeau, Judith Ray, Alison Ince, Gail Harvey, LCdr (ret'd) Terry Christopher, Ray Bedard, Jenny Miller, Steve Nash, Don Chabot, John Soffe, Jamie and Tony Edwards, Kim Smith, Kristy Smith, Tony Gabriel, Gerry Organ, J. J. and Donna Hilsinger, The Town of Terrace Bay, Chris and Tim Potter, Richard Getz, Lori Lee Calhoun, Joe Warmington, Paul Cox, Jim Buttici and Alison Stoneman, Craig Gardner, Peter Martin, Jack Creed, Peter Sutton, Karl and Jonathon Brown, Lennie Gallant, Janet Taylor McCaig, The Boon Family, Joe Barkovich, Bryan Wyatt, John Cameron, Cathy Alex, the Sciberras Family, the staff of the Thunder Bay Terry Fox Monument, Nigel and Cheryl Gordijk, Donna White, Andrew Iler, Mike Sullivan, Ray and Betty Laukkanen, BJ Cook, Julie Premo, Lisa Porcopl, the McCaig Family, Michael Flomen, Chris Coleman, Darren Wark, Jeff Sandler, Brock Kerby, Rob Reid, Josh Trager, Chris Vigars, Peter Sheremeta, Harold Kewley, The Turpis Group, Bev Norris, The McClew Family, Pete Charlton, Doug Lamb, Ed Rice, Paul Ski, Shane Harvey, Joan Gibb, John Kernaghan, Neil Tubb, Lou and Sandra Turco, Richard Guinan, Linda Fine, Town of Madoc Archives, the City of St. Thomas, a great place to grow up.

A special thanks to Terry Foxers, the ultra-supporters of Terry, such as Glemena Bettencourt who I enlisted to help collect donations and who travelled on and off with us for a while and thankfully kept many artifacts and photos from the journey. Dear friends who have fought cancer bravely with never ending hope and positivity, Michelle Fuller and Landi Lynch-Groenendyk. Jason Helmond, "I'm not disabled, I'm able," is a shining example of community involvement in his home town of Barrie, and I'm proud to call him my friend.

My mother and father, Jean and Gord Vigars, who put up with a bold brazen brat and allowed his crazy imagination to flourish (as if they had a choice) as well as my brothers John and Bob and my partner in childhood crime, sister Beth. Family makes you who you are.

Thank you to the school teachers across Canada and around the world who, for the last forty-three years, have kept Terry's legacy alive. Using Terry as an example, they have taught their students about the importance of community service, having hope when sometimes there was none, and demonstrating that dreams can come true with hard work and determination. In addition, a big thank you to the local run organizers across Canada who keep Terry alive every second Sunday after Labour Day. Your countless volunteer hours make all of you heroes.

Thank you to a very special person and dear friend, Paddy Wales. Without her support, guidance, and editing prowess, this publication would not be possible. I have known Paddy for over twenty-five years and I am particularly proud of working with her as she spearheaded a community effort to create the Sunshine Coast Botanical Garden in Sechelt, BC. Transformed from an abandoned tree farm, it has grown into and ecological jewel, a living legacy of her hard work and generosity.

ACKNOWLEDGEMENTS

In closing I want to acknowledge all those who have been touched by cancer, particularly those who may be fighting right now as you read this book. Great advances in research, funded by the millions raised by Terry, have made treating the disease much more successful. Still, there is a long road ahead. Please support the Terry Fox Foundation with your donations.